ARCHITECTURAL
LABORATORIES

ARCHITECTURAL LABORATORIES GREG LYNN AND HANI RASHID

NAi PUBLISHERS

CONTENTS

INTRODUCTION

MAX HOLLEIN

The present state of our urban situation cannot be solely addressed by its infra-structure or physical orientation. Our environment has to be understood as an ever-growing organism, influenced by every vector defining our society. New technologies, as well as the overall and instant availability of information, not only transform our daily life and routine, but also redefine the notion of the city itself. Recognizing urban structures as process-oriented, non-static, fluid environments requires an experi-mental and all-encompassing architecture that is physical, virtual and dynamic in its very condition.

Hand in hand with this development the professional title 'architect' is today as unclear as that of, for instance, 'doctor.' Under its guise a whole range of new and different professions can be found, of which ever fewer are concerned with the actual realization of physical, three-dimensional buildings. On the other hand, today more than ever architecture and architects are in the media focus. Public role, media pres-ence and professional presentation are, for better or worse, part of the architectural profile. Thus the use of the fashionable word 'hybridity' for the latest designs can also be regarded as symptomatic for the whole profession – the borders of practicing architecture are just as *fluid* as architecture itself. Young architects feel at home in a great variety of worlds. In virtual environments, just as in 'branding' and 'corporate identity' on the commercial level.

All in all this represents a clear instability of the traditional notion of the role of architecture and manifests a distinct desire for new content and tasks within the changing information society. It would be disastrous not to open up towards these developments in architecture schools. Opening up meaning not only to provide the adequate technological equipment of the training environment, but also to support a new relationship between the various areas of interest and a shift of emphasis in the teaching subjects and their mediation. Even more so since the borders between training and profession have become fluid. It is obvious that the most exciting moments are at present to be found in the experimental area between research and practice.

This publication pays tribute to these developments and as commissioner and curator of the US Pavilion at the VII Architecture Biennale in Venice two years ago,

I have also attempted to integrate this aspect into the entry. Deliberately I chose to emphasize a different kind of structure, one that did not feature an exhibition but hosted a production in progress, fostering active process rather than review, thus providing a breeding ground for new ideas, a gathering place for intellectual discourse, an architectural testing space and a contemporary research laboratory. The program, a publicly accessible workshop for two professors from two different universities and 25 students from the USA, presented the spectator with the mutated, digital process of work and research while also offering the students a platform – the Architecture Biennale and the US Pavilion – which was intended to be actually used: the interaction with visitors, press and colleagues, on site presentations and public debate, and even the cocktail reception on the roof terrace were all integrated elements of the Biennale concept. The US Pavilion was transformed into a workshop and forum for architectural discourse in order to investigate, produce and review a variety of architectural schemes. After this initial five-week period, the entire output remained on view until the end of the Architecture Biennale.

The program explored the application of new technologies in contemporary housing as well as new schemes for building archetypes such as the airport, performance center and stadium. For the research and design process, the students utilized advanced technologies that are commonly employed in multimedia, industrial design and special animation fields. These technologies were not used merely as the tool of architectural creation but as a recognition and absorption of them as defining factors of our complex living conditions and of our perception of time and space. Hence, these designs for our new urban environment were deeply rooted in and influenced by a thorough understanding of digital realities and their potential within a complex framework.

Hand in hand the program paid tribute to two of the most challenging and innovative personalities in the field of architecture and pedagogy of today. Hani Rashid and Greg Lynn are both not only on the forefront of architectural development but have from very early on in their careers been professors at important American universities with future-oriented architectural faculties, respectively the Graduate School of Architecture, Planning and Preservation at Columbia University in New York and the Department of Architecture and Urban Design in the School of Arts and Architecture at UCLA in Los Angeles. Besides pushing the boundaries within the design practice, institutionalized teaching became from the very beginning an integral part of their creative process. On the other hand they represented a completely innovative method of teaching and collaboration with the students, reflecting – not only in their 'paperless studio programs' the new definition of the architectural profession as described above, but also being on the very forefront of technological innovation. Greg Lynn at present teaches simultaneously at four – or five, it is hard to keep track – different faculties all over the world and uses the students results in the sense of a collaborative process quite openly for his own work – just as the students in return build upon his previous achievements. Besides a variety of 'real buildings' Hani Rashid (together with Lise Anne Couture) developed several three-dimensional information processing and representation systems, such as the Virtual Trading Floor of the New York Stock Exchange or the Virtual Guggenheim Museum website. As a logical development many of his students pursue new and non traditional forms of architectural practice from building design to virtual information environments.

Both Lynn and Rashid exemplify a new way of training students who possess an interdisciplinary, theoretical and practical methodology toward architectural research and creation. Although by different architectural approaches and formulations they prove an understanding of spatial configurations and building complexes that goes way beyond conventional geometrical definitions. Developing a play between the static physical and ever-changing ephemeral spaces, areas such as technology, animation or digital realities do not simply represent a means or tool, but an integral part of the urban context and experience. On this basis, the outcome of architectural creation ranges from the fully tactile product to the all-encompassing but entirely virtual environment.

PROLOGUE

GREG LYNN

The UCLA students were given a research project that my office had been working on for two years that was catalyzed by a discussion with an automobile manufacturer regarding mass produced one-of-a-kind cars. We were invited to talk to them because they understood that architects were expert in the assembly of mass produced components to realize custom monolithic forms. They needed the geometrical and dimensional control of variation that they perceived architects had mastered. My office had worked on and off on this hypothetical issue regarding a house that could be manufactured using existing contemporary factory processes used by the auto industry. The UCLA students were given the limits of the endless variations of this house volume and they were asked to design interior elements that could also be designed and manufactured in a like fashion. They were given the following brief.

The Embryological Houses©™ can be described as a strategy for the invention of domestic space that engages contemporary issues of brand identity and variation, customization and continuity, flexible manufacturing and assembly, and most importantly an unapologetic investment in the contemporary beauty and voluptuous aesthetics of undulating surfaces rendered vividly in iridescent and opalescent colors. The Embryological Houses employ a rigorous system of geometrical limits that liberate an exfoliation of endless variations. This provides a generic sensibility common to any Embryological House, while at the same time no two houses are ever identical. This technique engages the need for any globally marketed product to have brand identity and variation within the same graphic and spatial system; allowing both the possibility for novelty and recognition. In addition to design innovation and experimentation, many of the variations in any Embryological House come from an adaptation to contingencies of lifestyle, site, climate, construction methods, materials, spatial effects, functional needs and special aesthetic effects. For the prototyping stage six instances of the Embryological House were developed exhibiting a unique range of domestic, spatial, functional, aesthetic and lifestyle constraints.

There is no ideal or original Embryological House as every instance is perfect in its mutations. The formal perfection does not lie in the unspecified, banal and generic primitive but in a combination of the unique intricate variations of each instance and the continuous similarity of its relatives. The variations in specific house designs are sponsored by the subsistence of a generic envelope of potential shape, alignment, adjacency and size between a fixed collection of elements. This marks a shift from a Modernist mechanical kit-of-parts design and construction technique to a more vital, evolving, biological model of embryological design and construction.

Traditionally, Modern architecture, and especially domestic space, has been conceived as an assembly of independent parts, or a kit. The advent of industrialized assembly line fabrication and the marketing, distribution and assembly of these components conspired to support the generic kit-of-parts house. Likewise, the atmosphere of a limited advertising and media culture engendered a broad interest in simple generic structures of identity. The banal Modernist notion of generic housing involved the invention of a mass produced existence minimum structure to which customizations, additions, modifications and alterations could be performed by the addition of parts or components. This kit-of-parts identity was an appropriate technique for this cultural and industrial moment. With the progressive saturation of our imaginations by an advanced advertising media culture – which is becoming more and more creative, artistic and cunning in its techniques of creating desire for formal variation and uniqueness while maintaining brand identification – a more advanced generic identity is not only possible and probable but in fact necessary for contemporary domestic space.

The domestic envelope of every Embryological House is composed of 2048 panels, 9 steel frames, and 72 aluminum struts, networked together to form a monocoque shell; where each component is unique in its shape and size. Using design techniques of flexible manufacturing borrowed from the industrial, automotive, naval and aeronautical design industries, every house in the line is of a unique shape and size while conforming to a fixed number of components and fabrication operations. The form and space of the houses is modified within the predefined limits of the components. In addition, a change in any individual panel or strut is transmitted throughout every other element in the whole. A set of controlling points is organized across this surface so that groups of these generic panels can be effected to bud into more specific forms or what we call nodules. In every instance of this surface, there are always a constant number of panels with a consistent relationship to their neighboring panels. In this way no element is ever added or subtracted. In addition, every element is inevitably mutated so that no two panels are ever the same in any single or multiple configuration. These panels, with their limits and tolerances of mutation, have been linked to fabrication techniques involving computer controlled robotic processes. These include ball hammered aluminum, high pressure water jet cutting, flexible scissor lift molded glass fiber and resin panels, plastic roto-molding, vacuum-formed PETG plastic and three axis CNC milling of wood and composite board. In this way the limits and numerical constraints of computer controlled robots is also built into the software giving the panels their limits of size and shape. Every element is mutated so that no two panels are ever the same and so that no area of the interior is ever identical to any other area on the surface. The volume is defined as a soft flexible surface of curves rather than as a fixed set of rigid points.

Every Embryological House is designed as a flexible curvilinear surface. Their voluptuous fenestration, apertures, openings, and orientation to light, air, human and mechanical penetration occur through a technique of curvilinear shreds, louvers and pores that derive from the topology of their surfaces. Window and door openings are not cut into the surface of the Embryological House. Rather an alternative strategy of tears, shreds and offsets in their soft geometry is invented. Any dent or concavity of surface provides an opportunity for domestic occupation and the integration of apertures into the surface.

The surface envelopes are connected to the ground so that any alteration in the object is transmitted outward into the landscape. For instance, a dent or concavity in the envelope generates a lift or plateau in the ground. In this way a deformation in the object has a corresponding effect on the field around it, facilitating openings, views and circulation on a potential site. The houses are made to visually float on the site where an upper level volume is supported on vertical columns above the site. The landscape is pulled upward at the two poles of the house generating a mound garden that rings the house. The houses are adaptable to a full range of sites and climates. The minimum requirement for any site is a 100 foot diameter clear area with less than a 30 degree slope for the house and its surrounding gardens. A sea of mounds planted with alternating strips of decorative grasses surrounds each house. Nestled within these wave mounds, an undulating berm of earth receives the house. The berm slopes from the lower level to the upper level of the house in order to meet the front and back entries. The house appears to be buried in the ground from some orientations while appearing to float above it from others. Wherever the exterior form of the house is indented, a corresponding garden pod is formed, off of which a formal garden flows. These microclimate pods with their corresponding formal gardens are ringed by a perimeter of drift gardens that feather into the wave landscape of grasses.

Pure research through grants and exhibitions spur research topics such as the Embryological House. Once the parameters of these research topics are formalized

I move them into the academy and work with students on more specific architectural principles. For example, morphologies of 'blebs,' 'teeth,' 'flowers,' 'isoparm apertures,' 'structural matrices,' 'intricate texture,' and 'inflections and gastrulations' were all issues that emerged from the design of the Embryological House and were given to the UCLA students as paradigms for the interior design. These eight principles are the formal, geometrical, morphological issues that became the core research for the students as well as being recurrent techniques used in the design and construction of commercial projects undertaken by my office. There is a more or less linear transfer of techniques from exhibitions to teaching and finally into commercial practice. These eight morphological principles were first formulated through research funded by exhibitions and it then determined the intellectual, formal, stylistic, atmospheric and technical context for both the American Pavilion exhibition of UCLA student work and recent commercial projects in my office.

variation

BLEBS

GREG LYNN

A 'bleb' is a term used by designers to describe a curve, or a surface made of a network of curves, that intersects itself. Blebs, like all geometric conchoids and folium, result whenever a curve is offset along the direction of its normals beyond the virtual radius of its curvature. Mathematical instances of blebs are Freeth's Nephroid, the Folium of Descartes, the Limacon of Pascal, the Leminiscate of Bernoulli, Hypotrochoids, Strophoids or any other involutes or pedal curves. When curve networks are used to define a surface, then these self-intersections become a source of volumetric enclosure within the logic of a surface.

Soft Ball Project, Architectural Laboratories, Venice Biennale, Venice, Italy (2000)
Computer rendering of three soft balls inside Embryological House

__LASER_CUT_STYRENE_PLASTIC___COMPUTE

Soft Ball Project

The *Soft Ball Project* is a partition system for the Embryological House that embodies a sensibility of contemporary domesticity and corporeality that expresses voluptuousness, dynamism, animism, vitality,

and sensuality through light, texture, structure, and shape. As objects, the partition balls do not move and function under the pretense of an independent body, but maintain a self-indexed form that registers gravity and the human body.

The true 'organicism' of these object-bodies derives from their formal conception as differential, non-reducible wholes positioned in an environment with sibling variations. In the case of the *Soft Ball Project*, a generic sphere is divided into

six pleated panels which together create a tightly-seamed, self-supporting double skin. Equipped with a minimal skeleton and animated in the design space of the software, the primitive ball limits each iteration according to the

Soft Ball Project, Architectural
Laboratories, Venice Biennale,
Venice, Italy (2000)
Computer rendering of three soft
balls nesting on the Embryological
House's undulating floor

Plastic Flowers, Architectural Laboratories, Venice Biennale, Venice, Italy (2000)
^ Exterior view of an Embryologic House with a Plastic Flower bleb
^> Side view of an Embryologic House with a Plastic Flower enclosure

RENDERING_ _ _CNC_MILLED_ACRYLIC_PLASTIC

same set of parameters. Bending, slumping, colliding, or other such responses to contextual forces (including gravity) are indexed over the whole surface in such a way that a stretch or splay in one area is matched by compression in another. Their 'softness' indicates not a continuous mobility but rather the ability to be shaped in response to a given environment as well as to accommodate issues of aperture, fenestration, and seaming through surface manipulations and material variations. Entirely serialized, the process of fabrication is easily repeatable and may be adjusted according to variable seasonal or use conditions. (>> page 57 and 72-73)

Plastic Flowers
(>> page 64-66)

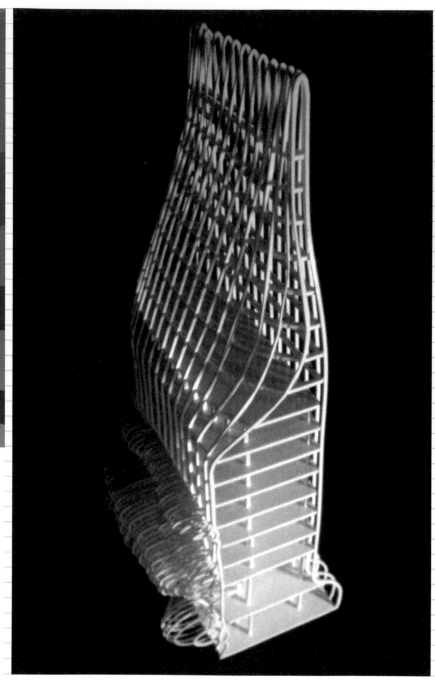

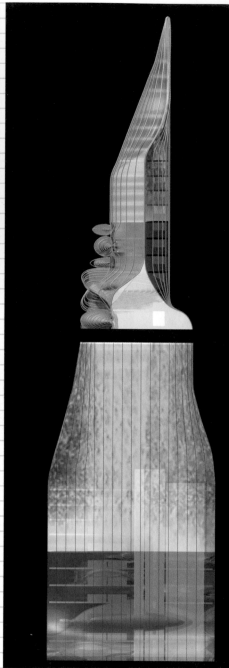

_COMPUTER_PLOTS___CNC_MILLED_LOW_DEN

The Eyebeam Atelier Museum of Art and Technology (competition entry)

The Eyebeam Atelier Museum of Art and Technology is an opportunity to build an icon and symbol not only for the state of art and technology, but also to create a monumental membrane between the physical and electronic world. It is now economically and technically viable to understand the surface of a building as being more valuable than its interior. The tower is a medium in itself, another channel for broadcasting. It joins the skyline as a permanent installation. By intricately folding this media skin at its base, spatial pockets are created that act as portals for pedestrians and museum visitors.

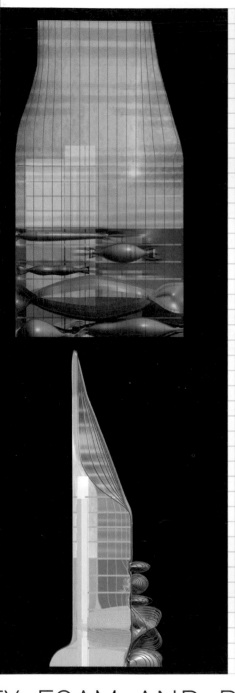

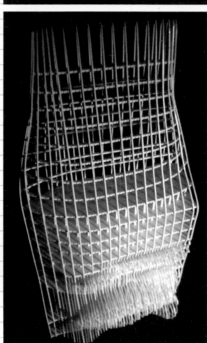

**Eyebeam Atelier Museum of Art and
Technology (competition entry)
Chelsea District, New York, NY (2001)**
^ Perspective view of lower levels
from the northeast
< Study model of curtain wall,
structure and cores, 1" = 1' scale
<< East, north, west and south
elevations clockwise from upper left
<<< Study model of curtain wall,
structure and cores, 1" = 1' scale

Y_FOAM_AND_PLASTER_ _ _CNC_MILLED_MULT

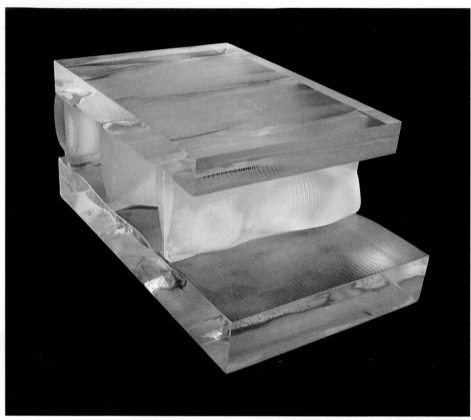

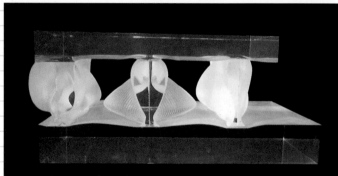

Extension of St. Gallen Kunstmuseum
(competition entry), St. Gallen, Switzerland (2002)
Two views of clear massing model, 1:150 scale

Rendel + Spitz Bleb Prototype 1
Cologne, Germany (2002)
Wall mounted installation

_ DENSITY_FIBERBOARD_ _ _ CAST_ALUMINIUM_

Extension of St. Gallen Kunstmuseum (competition entry)

The St. Gallen Kunstmuseum is unique because it combines, in the same structure, a natural history museum with a cutting edge contemporary art museum. The constraint that the existing building could not be touched or altered suggested a subterranean connection to the existing galleries. Two stories above this lower level extension we floated the archive and support spaces. This produces a monumental gateway to the adjacent park with the roof of the lower level extension acting as a plaza. Sandwiched between the outdoor ceiling and the plaza we located three special gallery volumes that are visible both from the city and from the park. (>> page 68)

Rendel + Spitz Bleb Prototype 1

This temporary installation for the Cologne Furniture Fair is part of a design collection of functional sculpture developed with the Max Protetch Gallery in New York. It shares the space with installations by Ross Love-

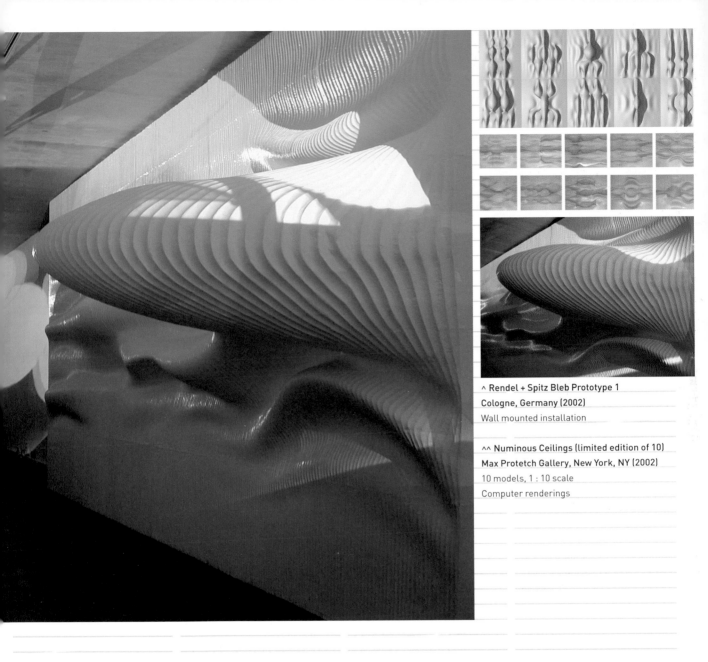

^ Rendel + Spitz Bleb Prototype 1
Cologne, Germany (2002)
Wall mounted installation

^^ Numinous Ceilings (limited edition of 10)
Max Protetch Gallery, New York, NY (2002)
10 models, 1 : 10 scale
Computer renderings

ACUUM_FORMED_PLASTIC_AND_POWDER_COAT

grove and Takejun Yoshioka. With their installations it shares qualities of animation in its surface pattern, texture, rhythm, undulation, form and shape. Unlike the relatively shallow relief of Horta and Sullivan's decorative surfaces – which

also emerged from new modes of manufacturing and fabrication, in their case at the turn of the last century – our deep relief surface is of a sufficient depth and scale that it has spatial consequences. Large panels of foam were laminated and

formed by a five axis router with a large diameter cutting tool.

Numinous Ceilings

The Numinous Ceilings are part of a collection of one-of-a-kind industrially produced objects that range from the scale of

architecture to furniture. The ceilings are 10' by 11' intricately textured, translucent, backlit, formed surfaces that are ceiling mounted in aluminum frames. Each ceiling has a unique shape and texture that is part of a general family of ten in the edition.

TEETH

GREG LYNN

The connection of disparate surfaces by co-planarity or blushing generates 'teething' across surfaces. The term teeth describes any connection between surfaces where two curves are tangent or have coincident control vertices. These connections allow movement, either literal or visual, across surfaces in a similar way that two level floors can be aligned in a co-planar fashion. At a smaller detail scale, teeth are a method of connecting disparate surfaces using their inflections in a similar manner to where interlocking joints are made through dado, mortise and tenon, or box cuts and interlocking joints. This technique of inflecting two surfaces together as a method for connecting them along coincident surfaces owes a great debt to Harry Cobb's theory of folding creases across disparate materials as a way of connecting materials into a monolithic curtain wall (see his essay 'Notes of Folding' in the 1994 issue of A.D. #102 titled *Folding in Architecture*).

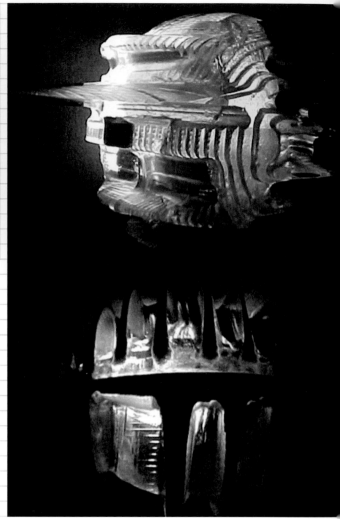

Tadpoles, Architectural Laboratories, Venice Biennale,
Venice, Italy (2000)
^ Lighting effects are produced by the cross-pollination
of geometric excavation and material chemistry
^> An index of effects is created by varying the milling
techniques and material recipes
> Portions of the mold remain to form a cradle of opaque
ligaments encapsulating the transparent resins

ED_ALUMINIUM___PLASTER_BASED_RAPID_PRC

Tadpoles

Through the use of CNC milling techniques, we are able to unify material, pattern, form, and marketry. Each component of the *Tadpoles* is milled as multiple profiles containing structure, material transparency, and void. In addition, the tool artifacting at every increment results in a unique patterning system. The tool artifacting pattern emerges and submerges by controlling adjustments in the building code. Incredimental changes in the cut line length reveal the history of the piece's production while simultaneously creating a vast index of effects. The result is a codependence of computer modeling and CNC milling techniques.

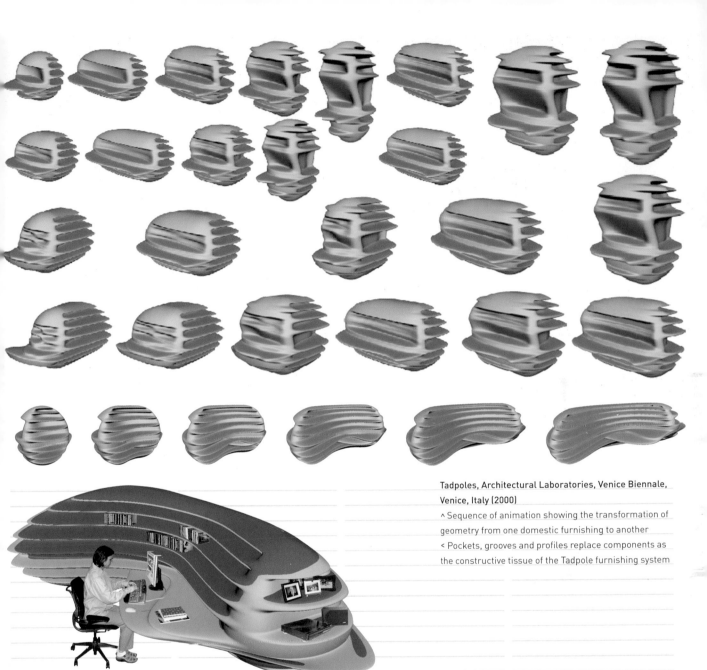

Tadpoles, Architectural Laboratories, Venice Biennale, Venice, Italy (2000)
^ Sequence of animation showing the transformation of geometry from one domestic furnishing to another
< Pockets, grooves and profiles replace components as the constructive tissue of the Tadpole furnishing system

TYPE___MULTI_DENSITY_FIBERBOARD_AND_CN

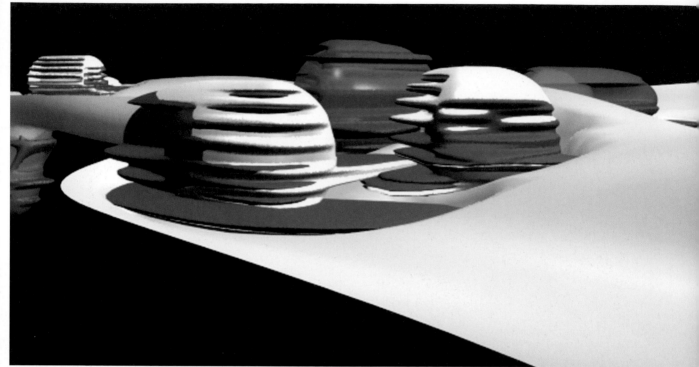

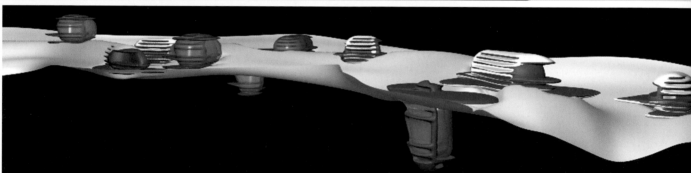

Tadpoles, Architectural Laboratories, Venice Biennale, Venice, Italy (2000)

Tadpole appliances emerge from the material surface of the generic Embryologic surface

C_MILLED_CLEAR_ACRYLIC___AIR_BRUSHED_C

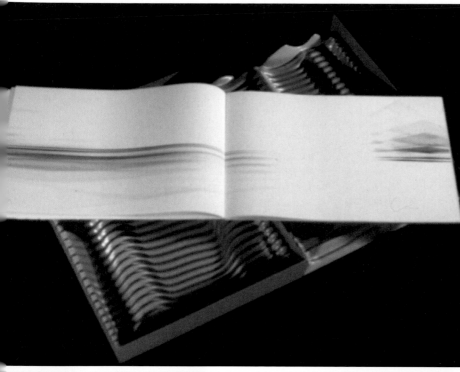

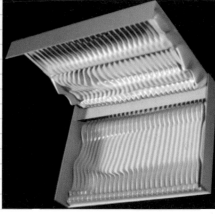

Visionaire #34 Case, *Visionaire Magazine*, New York, NY (2001)
Formwork

DR_SHIFT_AND_IRIDESCENT_ACRYLICS_ _ _SUF

Visionaire #34 Case Design

Visionaire #34 was edited by the new design director for Christian Dior Homme, Hedi Slimane. The theme of the issue was Paris; primarily environments and atmospheres that are global, technical, ambient, geometric, rhythmic, repetitive and visually cool. The metal and plastic case has no visible external articulation or hardware. The interior surface is designed with two complementary sets of 'teeth' that lock together to keep the case closed. The magazine floats on a system of waves in the core of the case. The minimal points of contact come together like two jaws. The two halves are designed with edges that can be tilted up and stood on their side and displayed as relief panels.

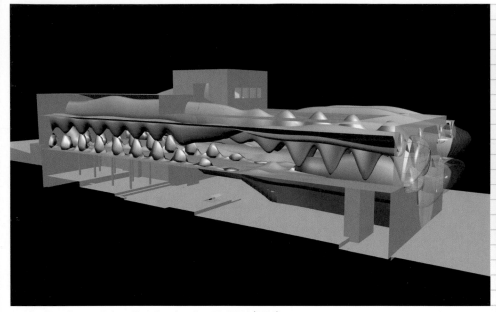

Lords on Sunset, Sunset Blvd., Los Angeles, CA 90046 (2001)
Interior perspective

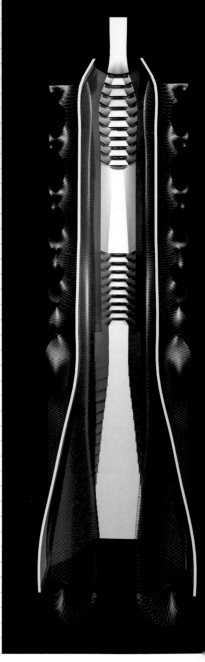

PER_FORMED_TITANIUM_ _ _VACUUM_FORMED_S

Lords Clothing store on Sunset
The interior and facade design for the new Sunset Boulevard location of Lord's Clothing compliments the store's reptile and leather skin clothing. Their clientele consists primarily of musicians and professional athletes and so the space functions as a retail store, lounge and club with a stage and bar at the upper level. The main structure of the building is an existing recording studio. The interior is designed as a textured and patterned surface that emerges from the floor and ceiling forming display enclosures and furniture. The building has a pedestrian entrance off Sunset Boulevard and parking space at the rear of the lot. A diagonal promenade through two levels terminates at the front and back facades with gem-like display windows.

Lords on Sunset, Sunset Blvd., Los Angeles, CA 90046 (2001)

^ Interior perspective

< Section perspective

RENE_ON_CNC_MILLED_MDF_TOOLS_ _ _LASER

FLOWERS

GREG LYNN

Flowering is a technique of transforming a tube into surface by slicing and flattening it, like the unfurling of the stem of a flower into a petal. Multiple stem and petal assemblages can be lathed, revolved, bifurcated and combined to form more complex surface constructions. In addition, volumes can be created by aligning surfaces along their edge seams and stitching them together into larger volumes that unfurl into independent tubular elements.

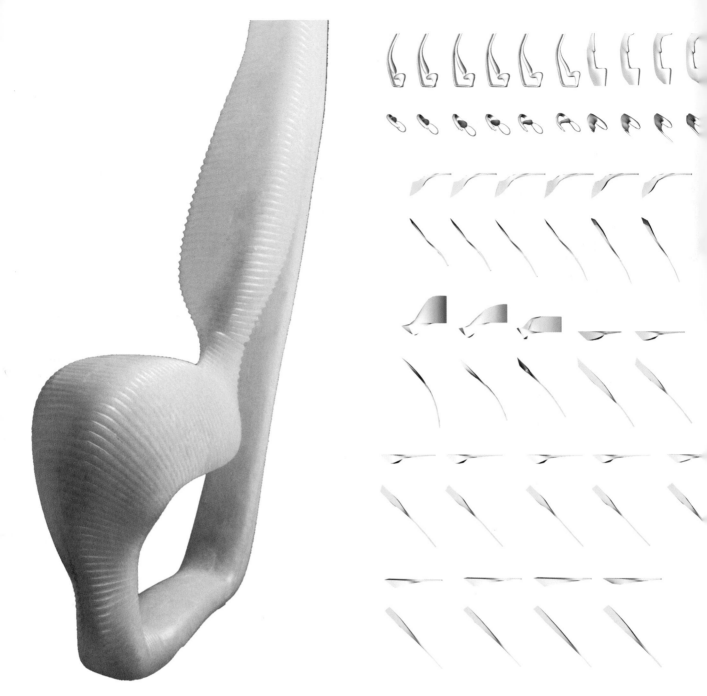

_CUT_STYRENE_SINTRA_AND_ALUMINIUM_FABR

X-Ray Wall System

Typically, furniture is considered to be distinct from the space in which it is situated. Similarly, architects often treat the floor and wall, interior and exterior, enclosure and fenestration as oppositional conditions. In contrast, our design for the Embryological House integrates structure, envelope and domestic landscape into a single system of subtly varying modules. From the shell of the house, a field of internal fins is derived. These fins are thickened, folded, and transformed according to a new geometry that resists the segmentation of functions exhibited in earlier paradigms. A single surface is responsible for structure, lighting, aperture, and spatial inflection. This multiple activated surface responds to specific tasks; from providing an enclosure for an appliance to providing a place for repose. Varying degrees of enclosure are achieved through a varying density of fins. A laminar material similar in flexibility, weight

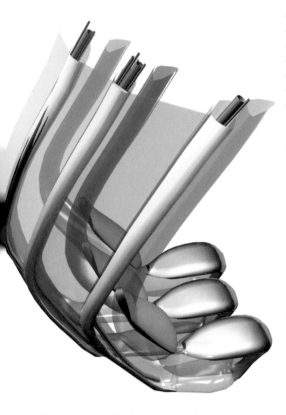

X-Ray Wall System, Architectural Laboratories, Venice Biennale, Venice, Italy (2000)
∧ Ensemble of individual chairs combined to provide a lounge condition. Exterior enclosure is defined by the subtle variations in curvature between similar elements of the X-Ray System
< The X-Ray System modulates between structure, lighting, furniture, appliance, and exterior shell
<< Fiberglass model of varying thickness and transparency produced from CNC milled patterns

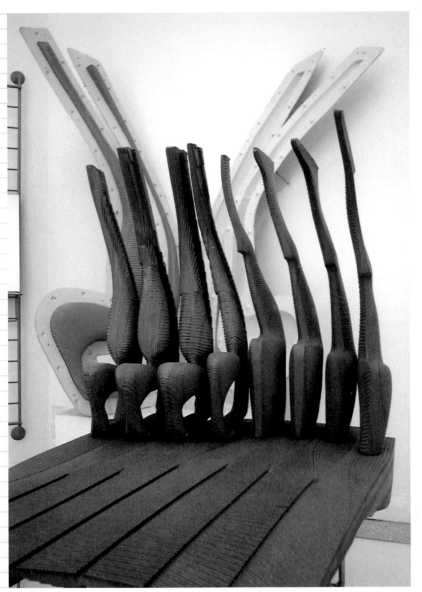

X-Ray Wall System, Architectural Laboratories, Venice Biennale, Venice, Italy (2000)
Ensemble of MDF models indicating the transition of structural fins from chair to appliance support

_ _COMPUTER_DRAWING_ _ _PETG_PANELS_DIG

and strength to boat sails and fiberglass hulls is used because it preserves the translucent nature of the structural fins. The striation patterns on the Kevlar and resin structural surface results from the artifacting of the machining process. These patterns are designed to take advantage of different types of cuts and lamination for visual and functional effect. Changing swells and folds in surface curvatures are accentuated by the milling operation. (>> page 44-47)

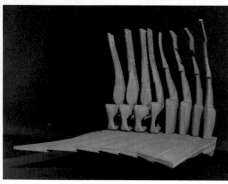

X-Ray Wall System, Architectural Laboratories,
Venice Biennale, Venice, Italy (2000)
^ Surface pattern study for X-Ray chair
< Ensemble of X-Ray fins and floor supports exploring
the relationship between program, tool path and form

GITALLY_PRINTED_VACUUM_FORMED_OVER_CN

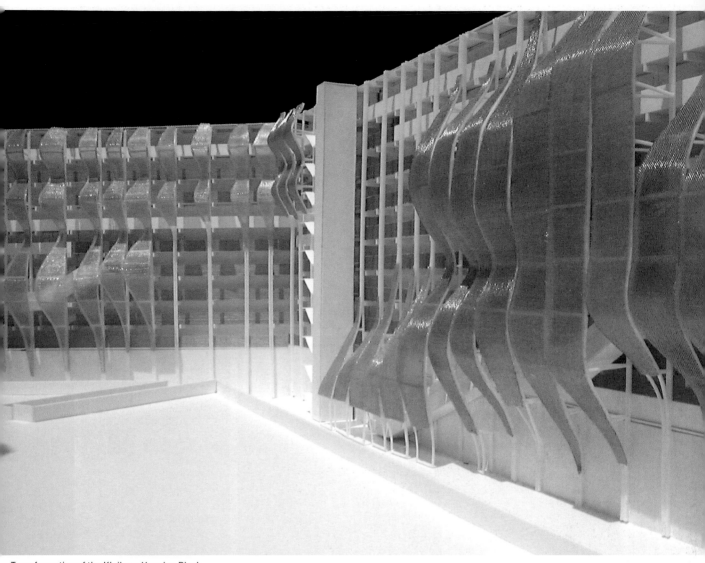

Transformation of the Kleiburg Housing Block
Bijlmermeer, Amsterdam, the Netherlands (2002)
Model view from the north, 1:100 scale

MILLED_FOAM_MOLDS___LASER_CUT_ACRYLIC_

Transformation of the Kleiburg Housing Block

This project radically transforms an existing 500 unit housing block, built in the early 1970s on the outskirts of Amsterdam. This project is a catalyst for the surrounding redevelopment; a model for the reuse of the other existing buildings; and a communications device for the housing corporation that owns the neighborhood. The design achieves both social and architectural diversity through the reduction of public space, the division of the block into manageable neighborhoods, the concentration of public access to these trunks of circulation, the multiplication of unit types, the grouping of unit types into bundles of homogeneous neighborhoods, and the design of the public spaces so that the neighborhoods have distinct identities. This is achieved through a mixture of new elevators and escalators. This building marks the first use of escalators in social housing. The new circulation is supported

Transformation of the Kleiburg Housing Block, Bijlmermeer, Amsterdam, the Netherlands (2002)

Perspective view looking northeast

AND_STYRENE_CNC_MILLED_EPOXICAL_AND_SI

by a series of over 150 uniquely shaped vertical steel trusses that are clad in a semi-transparent stainless steel fabric. Half of the existing units will be renovated and rented and the other half will be redesigned and sold as condominiums.

These units are larger and have a variety of unit plans including: loft, home office, duplex, garden, terrace, and office. The ground floor bicycle storage is moved vertically into bundles adjacent to neighborhood vestibules, making room for

ground floor housing. Over 30% of the public space and circulation is absorbed back into living space by removing the existing second level elevated street and many of the single loaded corridors. (>> page 49)

Transformation of the Kleiburg Housing Block
Bijlmermeer, Amsterdam, the Netherlands (2002)
Model view from above, 1:100 scale

RA___CNC_MILLED_MDF_WITH_METALLIC_ENA

MEL_PAINT___CNC_MILLED_ALUMINIUM_BLOC

Ark of the World

The Ark of the World is a new institution that celebrates the ecological diversity, environmental preservation, ecotourism and cultural heritage of Costa Rica. It is a tourist destination situated in a mountainous rain forest at the country's interior. It combines a natural history museum, ecology visitor's center and contemporary art museum. The design is inspired by the form, texture and color of the indigenous tropical flora and fauna. The building is oriented around a three-story central vertical space filled with representations of the Costa Rican environment terminating in a dome and observation canopy. Two floors of galleries for the exhibition of contemporary art inspired by the natural environment surround this vertical space. The ground floor of the building extends into a single story natural history museum.

(>> page 69)

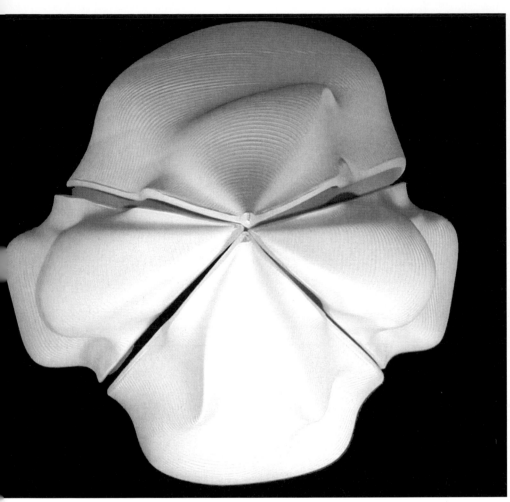

Alessi Tea and Coffee Piazza 2000, Verbania, Italy (2002)

^ Prototypes of super-formed titanium coffee and tea sets, full-scale

Ark of the World, Costa Rica (2002)

< Aerial view of model, 1:100 scale

<^ Section cut-away view of model, 1:100 scale

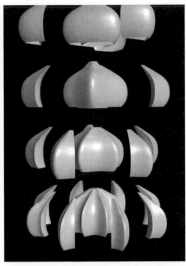

Alessi Tea and Coffee Piazza 2000
Verbania, Italy (2002)

^ Prototypes of super-formed titanium coffee and tea sets, full-scale
^^ Matrix of milled epoxy prototypes
^^^ Clusters of coffee and tea service items of different size and geometry generated from a matrix of curves

_ _ PETG_PANELS_VACUUM_FORMED_OVER_CNC

Alessi Tea and Coffee Piazza 2000

The Tea and Coffee Piazza 2000 is a mass-produced one-of-a-kind object. The incredibly light weight of the container gives it a space-age feel appropriate to the military aerospace methods of its manufacture. Each vessel is produced in a series of less than twelve and this allows each ensemble to be unique. Over fifty thousand unique ensembles have been designed for future production. The vessels are formed of thin metal titanium sheets using heat and pressure. Their surface retains the fine scale detail of the machined tool. The recently deregulated manufacturing process was invented for stealth airplane fabrication because of the necessary quality of surface detail and the accuracy of wall thickness.
(>> page 80-81)

ISOPARM APERTURES

GREG LYNN

Fenestration, vomitoria, doorways, and openings, in general, have been the bane of all designers that began to work with curve networks and spline surfaces. This is true of industrial, automotive, aeronautic and architectural design. Cutting a seam into a surface along the integral structure of its isoparms and splitting openings is one technique for maintaining a rigorous surface logic while achieving penetrations and apertures. Shreds, louvers, lozenges, eyes and other tapered directional figures result from this integral isoparm approach to openings in spline surfaces.

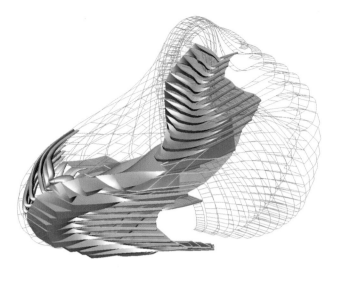

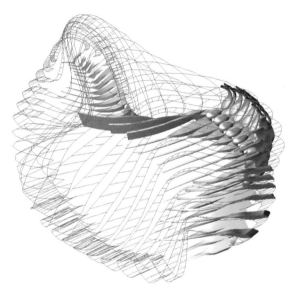

X-Ray Wall System, Architectural Laboratories, Venice Biennale,
Venice, Italy (2000)
^ Interior lighting effects of the Embryologic House are mediated by
the thickened transparency of the fiberglass wall system. Curvature
and material conditions combine to produce a palette of lighting effects
< The X-Ray System is a series of structural fins that transition from
structural rib to partition, seating, and floor support

MILLED_FOAM_MOLDS_PLASTIC_LAMINATE_COV

X-Ray Wall System

Typically, furniture is considered to be distinct from the space in which it is situated. Similarly, architects often treat the floor and wall, interior and exterior, enclosure and fenestration as oppositional condi- tions. In contrast, our design for the Embryological House integrates structure, envelope and domestic landscape into a single system of subtly varying modules. From the shell of the house, a field of internal fins is derived. These fins are thick- ened, folded, and transformed according to a new geometry that resists the segmentation of functions exhibited in earlier paradigms. A single surface is responsible for structure, light- ing, aperture, and spatial in- flection. This multiple activated surface responds to specific tasks; from providing an enclo- sure for an appliance to provid- ing a place for repose. Varying degrees of enclosure are achieved through a varying density of fins. A laminar mate- rial similar in flexibility, weight

house A

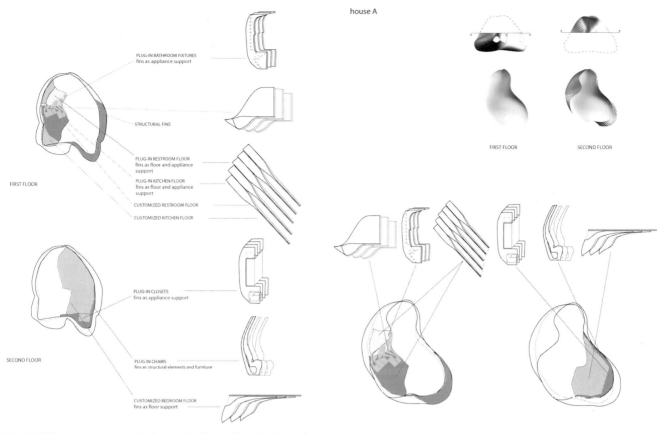

FIRST FLOOR

SECOND FLOOR

PLUG-IN BATHROOM FIXTURES
fins as appliance support

STRUCTURAL FINS

PLUG-IN RESTROOM FLOOR
fins as floor and appliance
support

PLUG-IN KITCHEN FLOOR
fins as floor and appliance
support

CUSTOMIZED RESTROOM FLOOR

CUSTOMIZED KITCHEN FLOOR

FIRST FLOOR

PLUG-IN CLOSETS
fins as appliance support

SECOND FLOOR

PLUG-IN CHAIRS
fins as structural elements and furniture

CUSTOMIZED BEDROOM FLOOR
fins as floor support

X-Ray Wall System, Architectural Laboratories, Venice Biennale, Venice, Italy (2000)

^ The system achieves flexibility through the subtle variation of form between one programmatic/ structural element and the next. No additional parts are added to the Embryologic House as all of the elements are extrapolations of the curvatures and flexation of the primary system

> A silicone jacket and fiberglass shell are created from the CNC patterns. The geometry of these molds is then translated back into a surface structure as a thin shell of chopped strand fiberglass impregnated with resin

ED_WOOD_RIBS_ _ _CNC_MILLED_MAHOGANY_ _

and strength to boat sails and fiberglass hulls is used because it preserves the translucent nature of the structural fins. The striation patterns on the Kevlar and resin structural sur-face results from the artifacting of the machining process.

These patterns are designed to take advantage of different types of cuts and lamination for visual and functional effect. Changing swells and folds in surface curvatures are accen-tuated by the milling operation. (<< page 34-36)

house B

house D

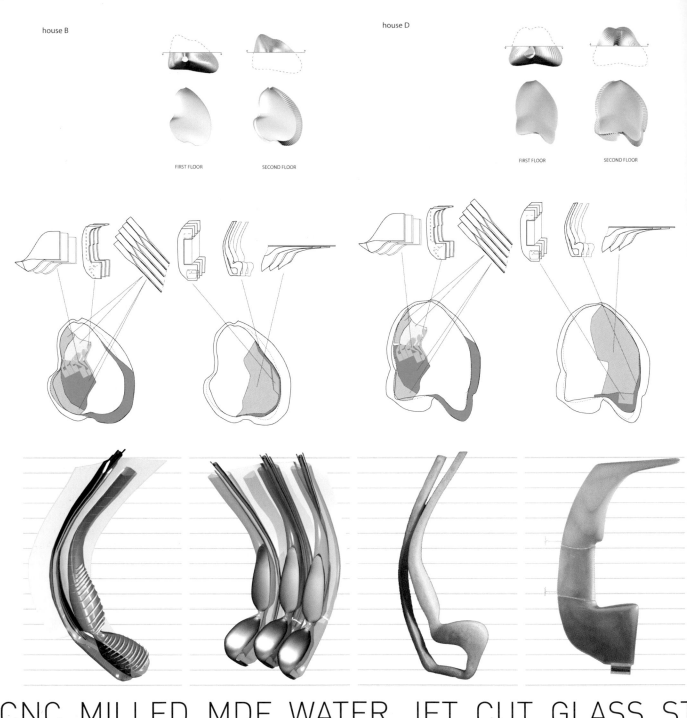

FIRST FLOOR

SECOND FLOOR

FIRST FLOOR

SECOND FLOOR

_CNC_MILLED_MDF_WATER_JET_CUT_GLASS_ST

house E

FIRST FLOOR   SECOND FLOOR

house F

FIRST FLOOR   SECOND FLOOR

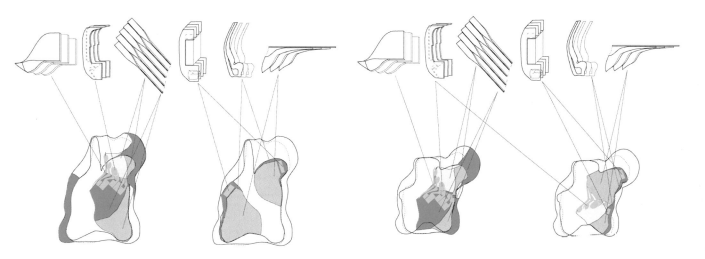

X-Ray Wall System, Architectural Laboratories, Venice Biennale, Venice, Italy (2000)
< Vacuum formed thermoplastic transforms the striations of the CNC tool path into modulations of light, reflection, and translucency
<< Hollow fiberglass model of continuously varying thickness produces different zones of stiffness, transparency, and curvature, and weight
<<< Ensemble of individual chairs combined to provide a lounge condition. Exterior enclosure is defined by the subtle variations in curvature between similar elements of the X-Ray System
<<<< Rendered image of X-Ray chair detailing the integration of elastomer cushioning, fiber optic cable, fiberglass shell, and exterior glazing system

X-Ray Wall System, Architectural Laboratories, Venice Biennale, Venice, Italy (2000)
^ Programmatic transformations are consistent between the various houses, but the form of such transformations is unique to the individual geometries of each condition

LESS_SHELVING_HARDWARE___CAST_URETHAN

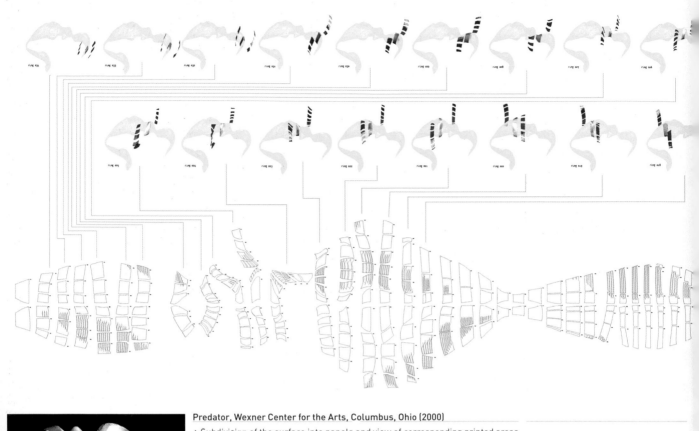

Predator, Wexner Center for the Arts, Columbus, Ohio (2000)
^ Subdivision of the surface into panels and view of corresponding printed areas
< Two perspective views

E___LASER_CUT_STYRENE_PLASTIC___COMPU

Predator

The Predator is the second collaboration between painting and architecture by architect Greg Lynn and painter Fabian Marcaccio. The two disciplines were digitally fused into an installation exhibited at the Wexner Center for the Arts. Digital paintings by Fabian Marcaccio are printed on large-scale clear plastic sheets. These sheets are vacuum formed with heat over 250 shaped foam panels. The printed computer-formed panels are then assembled to form an occupiable tubular surface. A CNC (computer numerically controlled) router carves the formwork. The tool paths are designed to accentuate this process for decorative effect. (>> page 59-61)

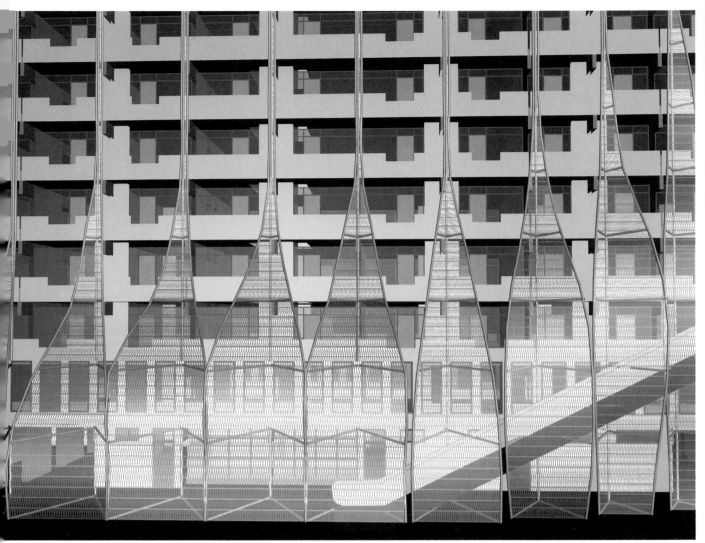

Transformation of the Kleiburg Housing Block, Bijlmermeer, Amsterdam, the Netherlands (2002)
Perspective view looking northeast

R_RENDERING___CNC_MILLED_ACRYLIC_PLAS

Transformation of the Kleiburg Housing Block

The radical transformation of an existing 500 unit housing block, built in the early 1970s on the outskirts of Amsterdam, is achieved through a mixture of new elevators and escala-tors. This building marks the first use of escalators in social housing. The new circulation is supported by a series of over 150 uniquely shaped vertical steel trusses that are clad in a semi-transparent stainless steel fabric. Half of the existing units will be renovated and rented and the other half will be redesigned and sold as condominiums. These units are larger and have a variety of unit plans including: loft, home office, duplex, garden, terrace, and office. The ground floor bicycle storage is moved vertically into bundles adjacent to neighborhood vestibules, making room for ground floor housing (<< page 36-39)

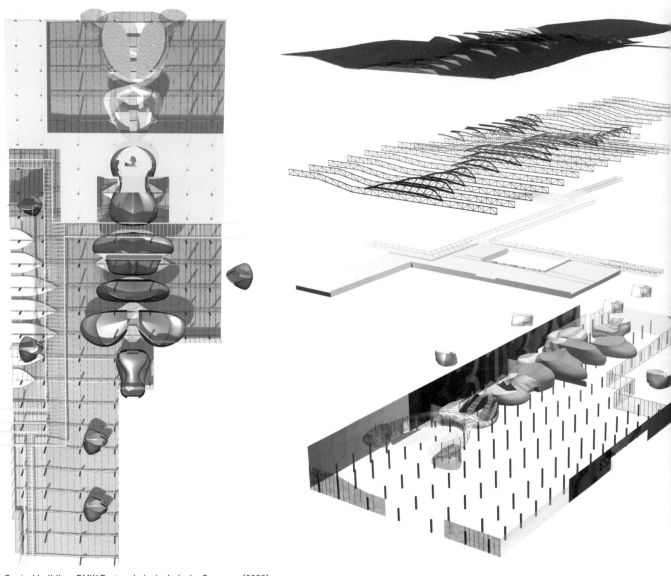

Central building: BMW Factory Leipzig, Leipzig, Germany (2002)

^ Worms eye view of central building

^> Rendering of main floor, audit rooms, mezzanine, skylights, and roof trusses

TIC___COMPUTER_PLOTS___CNC_MILLED_LOV

Central Building: BMW Factory Leipzig (competition entry)

The design of the Central Building for the new BMW car plant in Leipzig, Germany is sited between three factories with an exposed facade where workers and visitors enter. The client requests a flexible office and factory environment that the partially assembled cars pass through on elevated handling technology. The functions of inspection, quality assurance, research, measurement and visualization are centrally located in voluptuous metallic enclosures that communicate the materials, finishes, vocabulary and technical realization of BMW automobiles. These metallic volumes are located below a system of linear skylights that bring diffused daylight onto the factory floor. All functions not associated with the handling and manufacturing flow of cars are lifted above the ground level where they can have a spectacular vista.

(>> page 77-79)

Central building: BMW Factory Leipzig, Leipzig, Germany (2002)

^ Details of patterning on aluminium relief model of the reflected ceiling plan

^> Interior view of 1:250 scale model of central building

ENSITY_FOAM_AND_PLASTER___CNC_MILLED_

INTRICATE PATTERN, RELIEF AND TEXTURE

GREG LYNN

The principle of many CNC (computer numerically controlled) machines is controlling a cutting, deposition or routing head by moving it along a tool path. The conversion of a complex curved surface into a single line or a network of lines is the process by which a shape is sent to a CNC devise as a tool path. This process of converting a surface into a continuous traversing line presents opportunities for patterning, articulating and decorating a surface by designing the path and programming the machines to leave corrugated artifact patterns on the surface. The geometry of these tool paths is intricately related to the shape of the surface so that undulations in the pattern highlight and reflect the undulations in the form itself. In this manner an intensive decorative pattern emerges from the shape itself. In addition to designing moiré patterns of tool paths there is also the potential to map relief patterns on the surface that get accentuated by the tooling. The geometry can be displaced, or bump mapped, with images and paths so that the form itself is crisscrossed with finer grain veins and matrices.

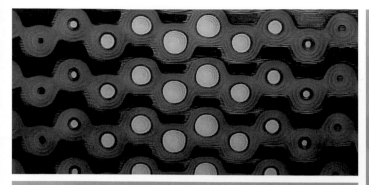

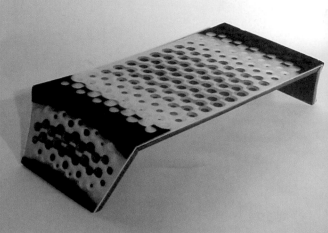

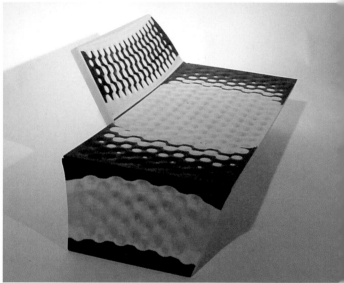

Tongue, Architectural Laboratories, Venice Biennale, Venice, Italy (2000)
∧ Detail of the three dimensional patterning produced on a generic
form to exploit various qualities of surface construction. The generative
nature of the dimensional texture provides for a flexibility in manufacturing
that could not exist when pattern is applied to surface as decoration
∧∧ Detail image of the material surface of Tongue construction

Tongue, Architectural Laboratories, Venice Biennale, Venice, Italy (2000)
A composite technique provides for the greatest flexibility in the Tongue system
Pattern and lamination are augmented by continuous modulations in the
curvature of the surface to produce complex relationships between visual and
sculptural effects

MULTI_DENSITY_FIBERBOARD_ _ _CAST_ALUMIN

Tongue

The *Tongue* is a surface for living. It is a multi-functional furniture system that transforms from a *chaise longue* to a shelf, to a coffee table; the *Tongue* design flips and folds in endless mutations based on one generic template. Every variation of size, pattern and fold direction is constructed from an articulated plane with a three-dimensional pattern that is removed from the material. In this way, pattern and strength are codependent; as the pattern dilates, the structure becomes increasingly thin; the deeper the bore, the larger the perforations. Varieties of use necessitate different pattern strategies. Sitting or reclining surfaces are developed with greater porosity than storage components.

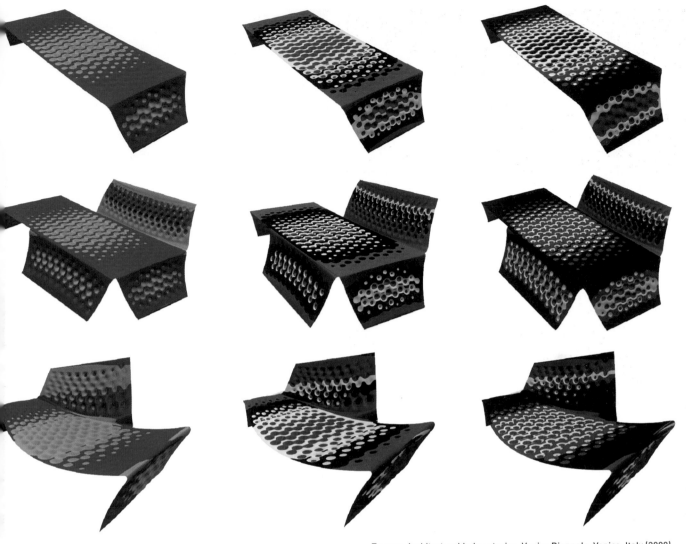

Tongue, Architectural Laboratories, Venice Biennale, Venice, Italy (2000)
Matrix of effects available in the Tongue system of construction

M_ _ _VACUUM_FORMED_PLASTIC_AND_POWDER

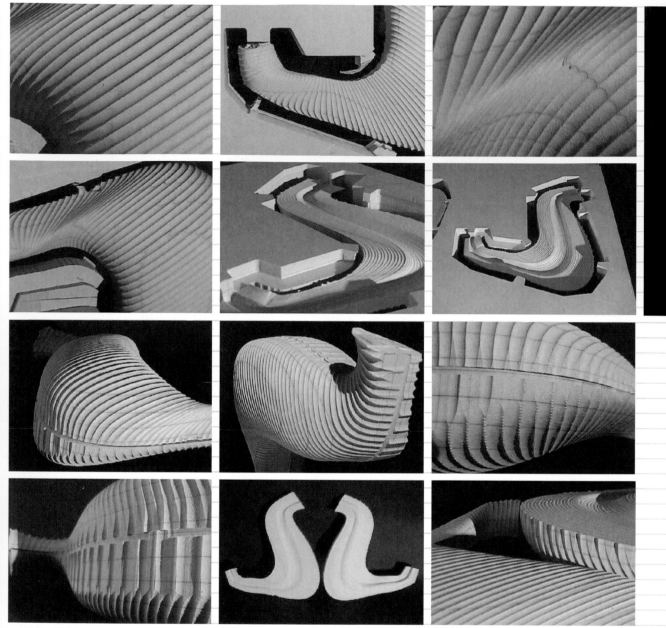

X-Ray Wall System, Architectural Laboratories, Venice Biennale, Venice, Italy (2000)
An uninterrupted tool path indexes the gradation of curvature that defines a surface of structure and programmatic opportunity

COATED_ALUMINIUM___PLASTER_BASED_RAPI

X-Ray Wall System
(<< page 34-36 and 44-47)

Softball Project, Architectural Laboratories, Venice Biennale, Venice, Italy (2000)
Details model of CNC milled mold surface

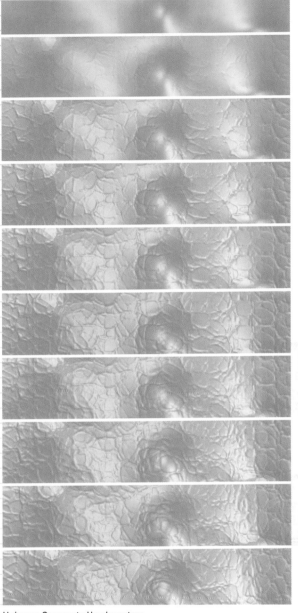

Uniserve Corporate Headquarters
550 S. Hope Street, Los Angeles, CA (2002)
Image sequence of surface patterning process

ROTOTYPE___MULTI_DENSITY_FIBERBOARD_AN

Soft Ball Project
(<< page 18-19 and >> 72-73)

Uniserve Corporate Headquarters

The new headquarter offices of Uniserve Corporation is a 4,500 square foot space downtown in a corporate high rise. Floating in the center of this loft like space is a long, translucent, plastic enclosure that houses a large conference room at one end and a smaller meeting room at the other. The outer surface of the enclosure is an undulating textured plastic wall that provides illumination for the surrounding open spaces and limits visibility between the open work area and the enclosed offices. The interior layer of the conference room is a faceted glass enclosure for soundproofing purposes. It floats within the curvaceous and patterned plastic wall as a crystalline gem.

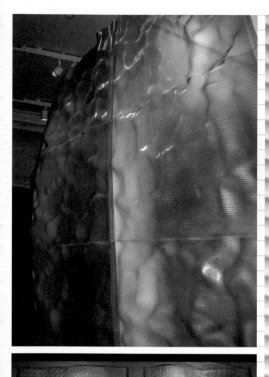

Uniserve Corporate Headquarters
550 S. Hope Street, Los Angeles, CA (2002)
^ Mock-up of two bays
^^ Model study of the conference room skin

Pretty Good Life Showroom
Stockholm, Sweden (1999)
Interior photograph

D_CNC_MILLED_CLEAR_ACRYLIC___AIR_BRUSH

Pretty Good Life Showroom
The showroom concept for PrettyGoodLife.com responds to the need for a mutable brand identity in a variety of contexts throughout the world. Given the same generic design technique, high degrees of variation can be produced for showrooms of various size and shape in different locales. The interiors are both customized and mass-produced using advanced computer controlled manufacturing processes and the control of design variations.

The existing spaces are built with gently bulging plaster walls, gradually sloping poured epoxy floors, aluminum metal trim, and frosted glass luminescent ceilings. Encased within this cleanly defined shell is a curvilinear volume that has a

_COLOR_SHIFT_AND_IRIDESCENT_ACRYLICS_ _ _

voluptuous undulating wood surface manufactured using CNC robots. Rather than a smooth surface, the texture of these panels is designed as a rippling surface that exploits the artifacting of the manufacturing robot. The undulations of the surface provide for both the projection of objects out from the wall and the nesting of smaller objects in niches. A system of stainless steel display pegs can be inserted across a network of receptacles embedded in the carved wooden blocks of the display wall. The reversible glass shelves have two differently curved profiles so that they can be aligned to at least two different positions on the wall. In this way the design achieves both a flexible and unique functional scheme within each showroom as well as a variety of shapes, sizes and configurations in different locations; all of which derive from a single design and construction strategy.

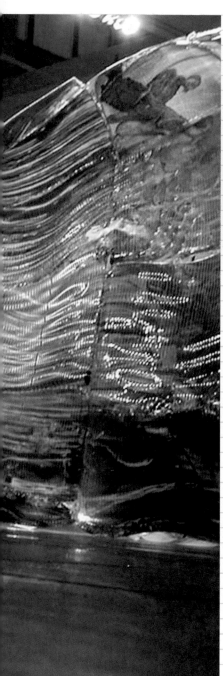

Predator, Wexner Center for the Arts, Columbus, Ohio (2000)
Gallery view

SUPER_FORMED_TITANIUM___VACUUM_FORME

Predator

The Predator is the second col-laboration between painting and architecture by architect Greg Lynn and painter Fabian Marcaccio. The two disciplines were digitally fused into an installation exhibited at the Wexner Center for the Arts. Digital paintings by Fabian Marcaccio are printed on large-scale clear plastic sheets. These sheets are vacuum formed with heat over 250 shaped foam panels. The print-ed computer-formed panels are then assembled to form an occupiable tubular surface. A CNC (computer numerically controlled) router carves the formwork. The tool paths are designed to accentuate this process for decorative effect. (<< page 48)

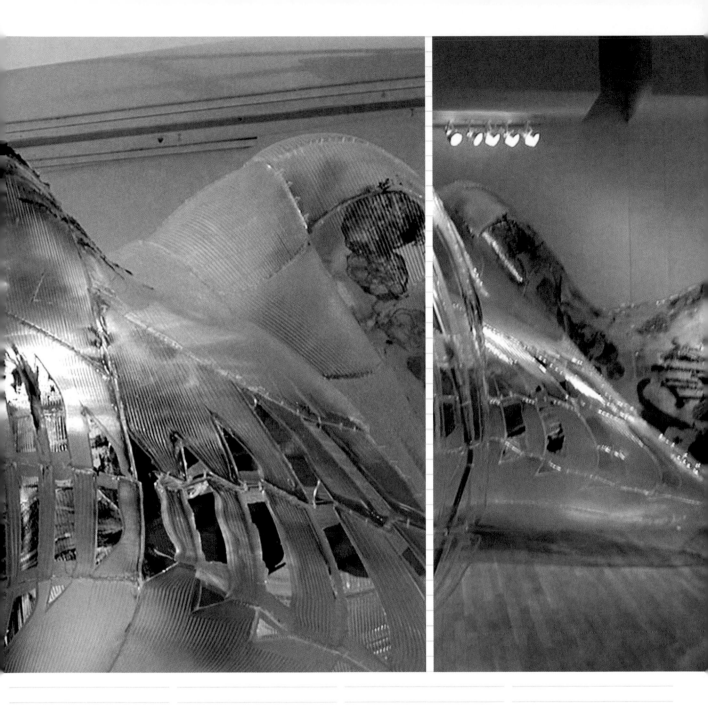

STYRENE_ON_CNC_MILLED_MDF_TOOLS_ _ _LAS

MATRICES

GREG LYNN

The composition and construction of a monolithic surface out of a collection of networked and interrelated components is perhaps the unique and intrinsic problem of architectural design and building construction. Using a numerically linked software program, the interrelations between elements can become intricate – intricate in the sense that each and every member is unique in its relationship to adjoining members and even to the entire organization of a surface. This is not just a variety of elements but the structural, harmonic and dimensional interdependency of components one to another in a rigorous and even hierarchical manner. Issues of tessellation, framing, monocoque shells, lattices and panel systems emerge from this research.

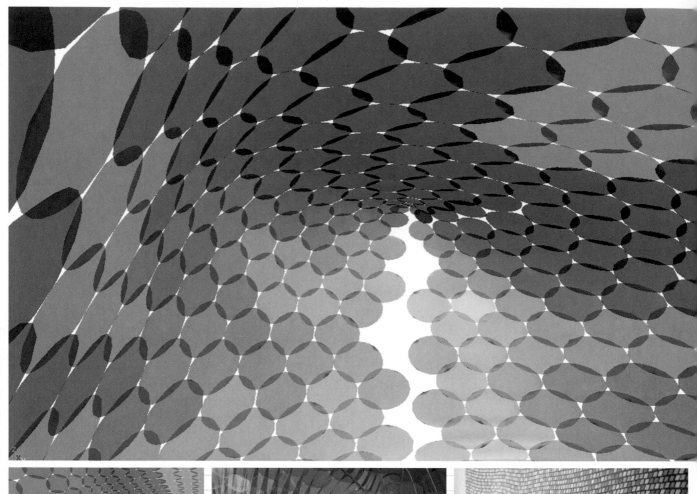

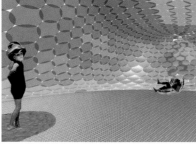

Plastic Flowers, Architectural Laboratories, Venice Biennale, Venice, Italy (2000)
Three interior views of Plastic Flower room
^> One-half of actual scale, mosaic mock-up of a section of a Plastic Flower floor

ER_CUT_STYRENE_SINTRA_AND_ALUMINIUM_FA

Plastic Flowers

The *Plastic Flower* envelopes recall the formal and structural properties found in nature through experimental and innovative building techniques and a hyper-synthetic materiality. This new strategy for surface paneling mediates between local environmental conditions and interior domestic space. The surface under investigation is the *bleb*, a small blister or air bubble; a formal result of placing the Embryologic House into the landscape. The space functions like a sunroom, as it mediates between inside and outside.

The bleb provides an opportunity to explore ideas of variation in composite surfaces. The bleb is covered with a non-modular panel system. The tiling pattern is rigorously based on the geometry of the surface. The regularity of the module disappears as dimensions shift slightly over the entire bleb. The result is endless variability in both shape and location of the bleb. The voluptuousness of

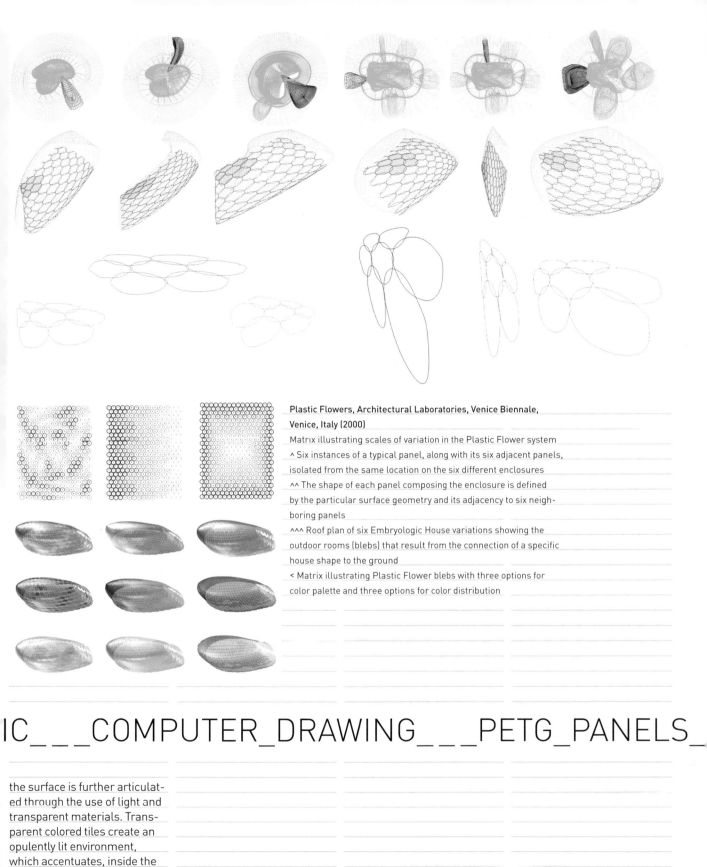

**Plastic Flowers, Architectural Laboratories, Venice Biennale,
Venice, Italy (2000)**

Matrix illustrating scales of variation in the Plastic Flower system

^ Six instances of a typical panel, along with its six adjacent panels,
isolated from the same location on the six different enclosures

^^ The shape of each panel composing the enclosure is defined
by the particular surface geometry and its adjacency to six neighboring panels

^^^ Roof plan of six Embryologic House variations showing the
outdoor rooms (blebs) that result from the connection of a specific
house shape to the ground

< Matrix illustrating Plastic Flower blebs with three options for
color palette and three options for color distribution

IC___COMPUTER_DRAWING___PETG_PANELS_

the surface is further articulated through the use of light and
transparent materials. Transparent colored tiles create an
opulently lit environment,
which accentuates, inside the
house, the temporal changes of
the environment. (<< page 19)

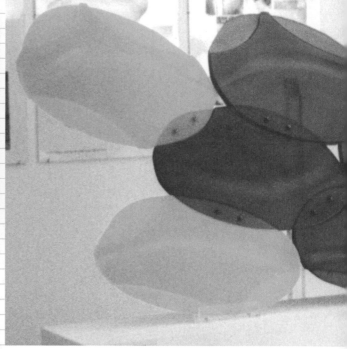

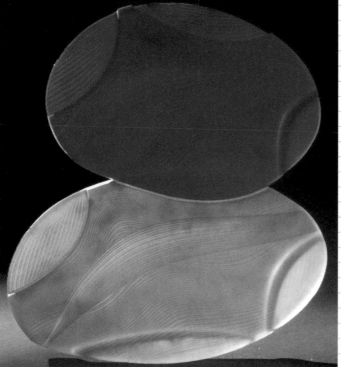

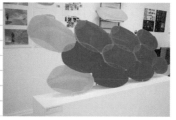

Plastic Flowers, Architectural Laboratories, Venice Biennale, Venice, Italy (2000)
One-half of actual scale, translucent acrylic mock-up of a section of a Plastic
Flower bleb

DIGITALLY_PRINTED_VACUUM_FORMED_OVER_C

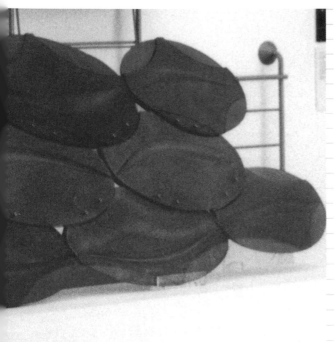

> Responsive Floor System, Architectural Laboratories,
Venice Biennale, Venice, Italy (2000)

Exploded axonometric view of responsive living surface

_MILLED_FOAM_MOLDS___LASER_CUT_ACRYLIC

Responsive Floor System

The *Responsive Floor System* tailors discreet uses, materials and utilities into a composite floor system that is the core organ of the Embryologic House. Its pod-like rooms and integrated furniture are receptacles for domestic activity. The pod platforms, furniture and services are highly customizable according to individual consumer desires and demands. Mass-produced consumer objects have previously been limited to generic or standard forms and dimensions due to both design and manufacturing limitations. The software driven sensibility of the *Responsive Floor System* and its optimization of CNC fabrication expands the possibilities for mass-produced domestic environments and harnesses a new type of architecture. The new envelope enables a customizable niche for architectural products that were once uneconomical in terms of mass-production. (>> page 73-75)

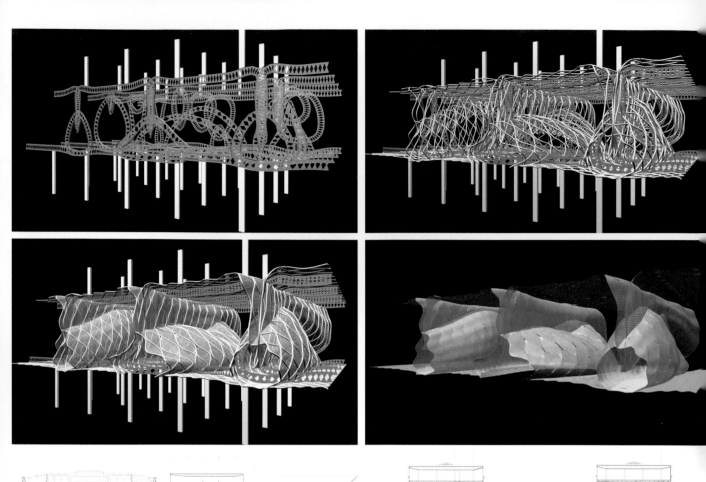

Extension of St. Gallen Kunstmuseum (competition entry), St. Gallen, Switzerland (2001)

∧ Sections through the gallery, storage, and mechanical spaces

∧∧ Four views of the structure, lattice, and skin systems interlaced to form the galleries for the expansion of the St. Gallen museum

AND_STYRENE_CNC_MILLED_EPOXICAL_AND_SI

Extension of St. Gallen Kunstmuseum (competition entry)

The St. Gallen Kunstmuseum is unique because it combines, in the same structure, a natural history museum with a cutting edge contemporary art museum. The constraint that the existing building could not be touched or altered suggested a subterranean connection to the existing galleries. Two stories above this lower level extension we floated the archive and support spaces. This produces a monumental gateway to the adjacent park with the roof of the lower level extension acting as a plaza. Sandwiched between the outdoor ceiling and the plaza we located three special gallery volumes that are visible both from the city and from the park. (<< page 22)

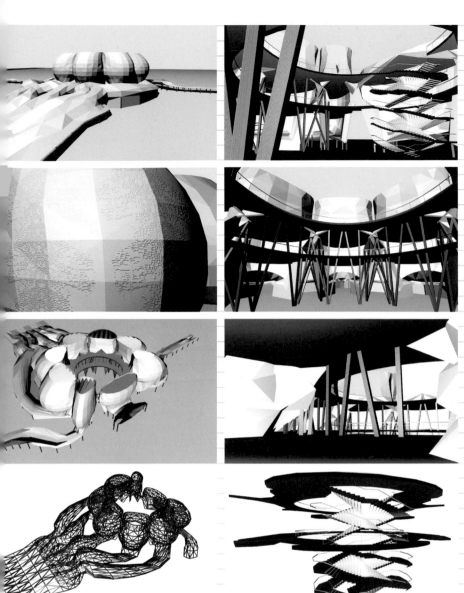

Ark of the World, Costa Rica, (2002)
Reflected ceiling plan

Ark of the World, Costa Rica, (2002)
Various computer generated views

RA___CNC_MILLED_MDF_WITH_METALLIC_ENA

Ark of the World

The Ark of the World is a new institution that celebrates the ecological diversity, environmental preservation, ecotourism and cultural heritage of Costa Rica. It is a tourist destination situated in a mountain-ous rain forest at the country's interior. It combines a natural history museum, ecology visitor's center and contemporary art museum. The design is inspired by the form, texture and color of the indigenous tropical flora and fauna. The building is oriented around a three-story central vertical space filled with representations of the Costa Rican environment terminating in a dome and observation canopy. Two floors of galleries for the exhibition of contemporary art inspired by the natural environment surround this vertical space. The ground floor of the building extends into a single story natural history museum.

(<< page 40)

INFLECTIONS AND GASTRULATIONS

GREG LYNN

The addition of singularities to otherwise generic and featureless surfaces is the sign of mastery over surface modeling software. Rather than participating in the space race for the first unarticulated featureless building that resembles most a computer rendering, the students were encouraged to explore surface articulation in terms of shape and pattern. Gastrulations, inflections, invaginations, pockets, dents, divots and other forms of shaping space through the modeling of a surface were explored. This included undulating landscapes and wall and ceiling elements forming spatial pockets and enclosures.

Soft Ball Project, Architectural Laboratories, Venice Biennale, Venice, Italy (2000)
Model of one sample softball enclosure system located within a section of an Embryological House interior

MEL_PAINT_ _ _CNC_MILLED_ALUMINIUM_BLOC

Soft Ball Project

The *Soft Ball Project* is a partition system for the Embryological House that embodies a sensibility of contemporary domesticity and corporeality that expresses voluptuousness, dynamism, animism, vitality, and sensuality through light, texture, structure, and shape. As objects, the partition balls do not move and function under the pretense of an independent body, but maintain a self-indexed form that registers gravity and the human body.

The true 'organicism' of these object-bodies derives from their formal conception as differential, non-reducible wholes positioned in an environment with sibling variations. In the case of the *Soft Ball Project*, a generic sphere is divided into six pleated panels which together create a tightly-seamed, self-supporting double skin. Equipped with a minimal skeleton and animated in the design space of the software, the primitive ball limits each iteration according to the

Responsive Floor System, Architectural Laboratories,
Venice Biennale, Venice, Italy (2000)
Plan view of living surface showing transparency of
materials and structural framing

Soft Ball Project, Architectural Laboratories, Venice Biennale, Venice, Italy (2000)
∧ Bedroom ball interior
∧∧ Three balls in the house interior

_ _PETG_PANELS_VACUUM_FORMED_OVER_CNC

same set of parameters. Bending, slumping, colliding, or other such responses to contextual forces (including gravity) are indexed over the whole surface in such a way that a stretch or splay in one area is matched by compression in another. Their 'softness' indicates not a continuous mobility but rather the ability to be shaped in response to a given environment as well as to accommodate issues of aperture, fenestration, and seaming through surface manipulations and material variations. Entirely serialized, the process of fabrication is easily repeatable and may be adjusted according to variable seasonal or use conditions. (<< page 18-19 and 57)

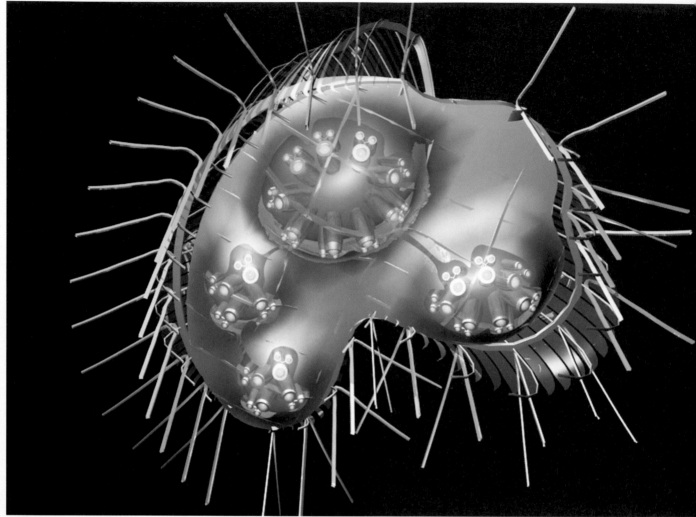

Responsive Floor System, Architectural Laboratories, Venice Biennale,
Venice, Italy (2000)
Underside view, overhead perspective, plan view and rendered section of
living surface

MILLED_FOAM_MOLDS_PLASTIC_LAMINATE_CC

Responsive Floor System

The *Responsive Floor System* tailors discreet uses, materials and utilities into a composite floor system that is the core organ of the Embryologic House. Its pod-like rooms and integrated furniture are recep-tacles for domestic activity. The pod platforms, furniture and services are highly customizable according to individual consumer desires and demands. Mass-produced consumer objects have previously been limited to generic or stan-dard forms and dimensions due to both design and manu-facturing limitations. The soft-ware driven sensibility of the *Responsive Floor System* and its optimization of CNC fabrication expands the possibilities for mass-produced domestic envi-

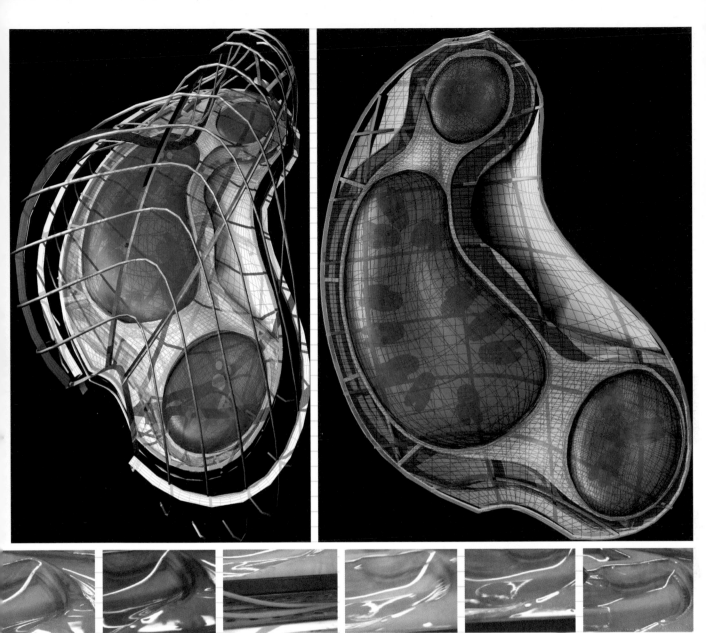

X-Ray Wall System, Architectural Laboratories, Venice Biennale, Venice, Italy (2000)

Sequence of images from vacuum forming process

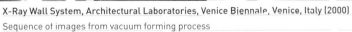

RED_WOOD_RIBS_ _ _CNC_MILLED_MAHOGANY_

ronments and harnesses a new
type of architecture. The new
envelope enables a customizable niche for architectural
products that were once uneconomical in terms of mass-production. (<< page 67)

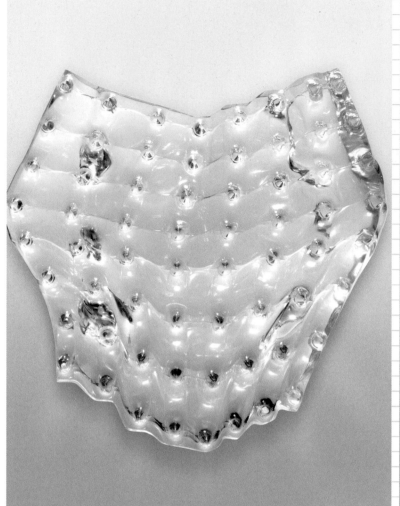

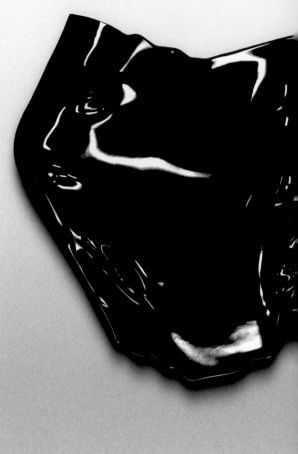

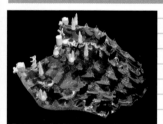

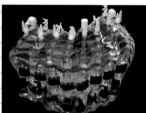

Chess Set for Deitch Projects, New York, NY (2001)

^ Photograph from above and below

< Clear urethane casting of chess board by
Greg Lynn FORM with pieces by Greg Foley

_ _ _CNC_MILLED_MDF_WATER_JET_CUT_GLAS

Chess Set for Deitch Projects
This design for a chess board was initiated by the design team ORFI (Organization for Returning Fashion Interest) to revisit the meaning of the game of chess from a contemporary point of view. These ideas are realized through objects that are related to the conventional and historic function of chess pieces. The board was designed as a landscape with volume and mass rather than as a plane. It rests on multiple undulations from below and the pieces come to rest on raised dimples that correspond to the conical cusps on the bottom of the pieces. The board was CNC manufactured in our office, first in wood, then in epoxical resin. From these positive forms, silicon formwork was formed and urethane objects were cast. There are three color options for the boards and the pieces: clear, black and white.

Central Building: BMW Factory Leipzig, Leipzig, Germany (2002)
∧ View from interior without roof, 1 : 250 scale
> Skylight shreds bring natural light to mezzanine and main floor of central building

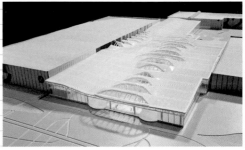

TAINLESS_SHELVING_HARDWARE___CAST_URET

Central Building: BMW Factory Leipzig (competition entry)
The design of the Central Building for the new BMW car plant in Leipzig, Germany is sited between three factories with an exposed facade where workers and visitors enter. The client requests a flexible office and factory environment that the partially assembled cars pass through on elevated handling technology. The functions of inspection, quality assurance, research, measurement and visualization are centrally located in voluptuous metallic enclosures that communicate the materials, finishes, vocabulary and technical realization of BMW automobiles. These metallic volumes are located below a system of linear skylights that bring diffused daylight onto the factory floor. All functions not associated with the handling and manufacturing flow of cars are lifted above the ground level where they can have a spectacular vista. (<< page 50-51)

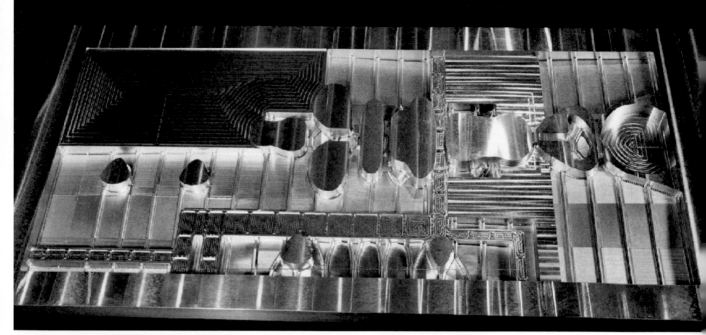

Central Building: BMW Factory Leipzig
Leipzig, Germany (2002)
^ Reflected ceiling plan model, 1:250 scale
< Detail of 1:250 model showing courtyards and
audit zones
<< View of main entrance to central building

HANE___LASER_CUT_STYRENE_PLASTIC___CO

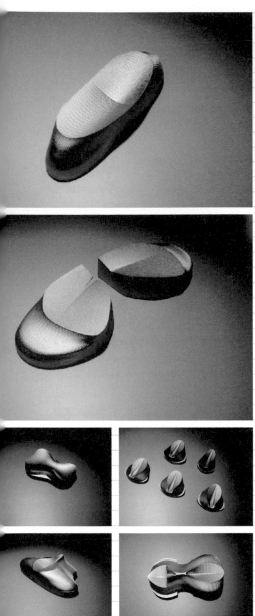

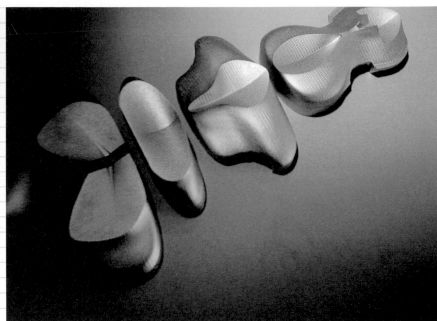

Central Building: BMW Factory
Leipzig, Leipzig, Germany (2002)
Studies of interior volumes,
1:250 scale

UTER_RENDERING_ _ _CNC_MILLED_ACRYLIC_F

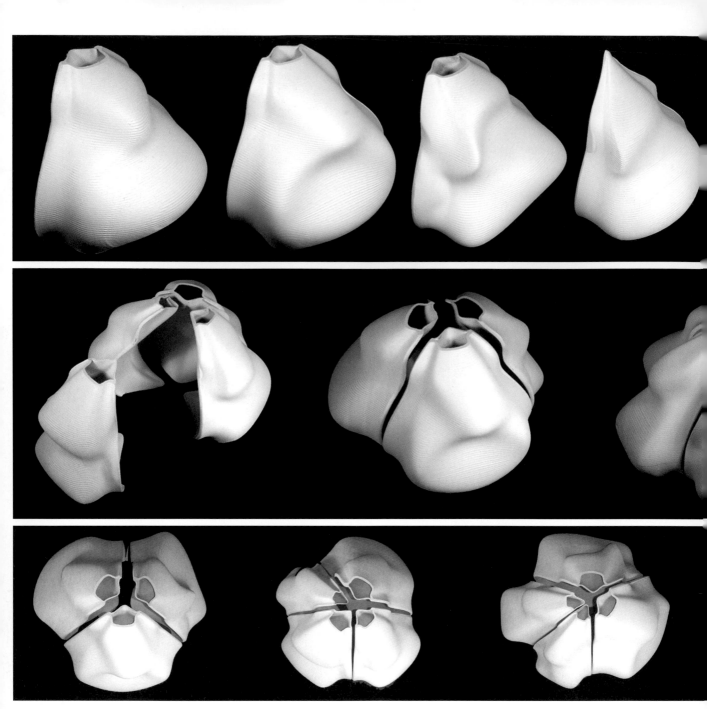

ASTIC _ _ _COMPUTER_PLOTS_ _ _ _CNC_MILLED_

Alessi Tea and Coffee Piazza 2000

The Tea and Coffee Piazza 2000 is a mass-produced one-of-a-kind object. The incredibly light weight of the container gives it a space-age feel appropriate to the military aerospace meth- ods of its manufacture. Each vessel is produced in a series of less than twelve and this allows each ensemble to be unique. Over fifty thousand unique ensembles have been designed for future production. The ves- sels are formed of thin metal titanium sheets using heat and pressure. Their surface retains the fine scale detail of the machined tool. The recently deregulated manufacturing process was invented for stealth airplane fabrication because of the necessary quality of surface detail and the accuracy of wall thickness. (<< page 41)

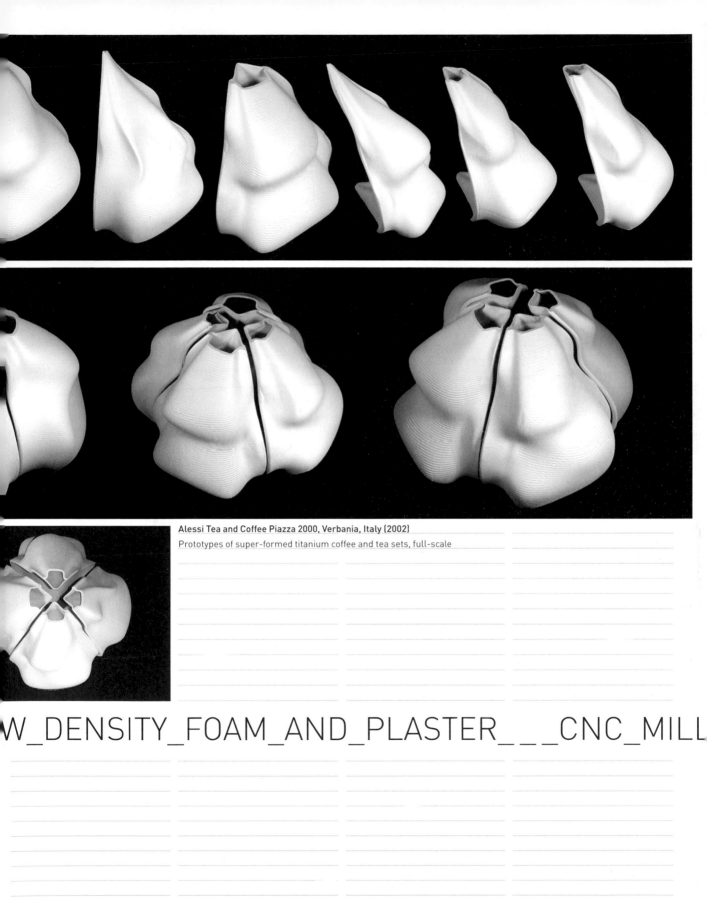

Alessi Tea and Coffee Piazza 2000, Verbania, Italy (2002)

Prototypes of super-formed titanium coffee and tea sets, full-scale

W_DENSITY_FOAM_AND_PLASTER___CNC_MILL

changing ephemeral spaces, areas such as te
do not simply represent a means or tool, but an
experience. On this basis, the outcome of arch
tactile product to the all-encompassing but entir

Max Hollein
U.S. Commissioner

rogram for the U.S. Pavilion has been dev
olomon R. Guggenheim Foundation.

by

telliStation

Line

Hani Rashid

Max Hollein

ogy, animation of digital realities
ral part of the urban context and
ral creation ranges from the fully
rtual
ein, U.
tional s
Flooring
bel Staff
za
nternation
Wavefront
s Krieble
and Chris
uadrivio
mous dor

MAX HOLLEIN IN CONVERSATION WITH HANI RASHID AND GREG LYNN

MAX HOLLEIN: First, I would like you to elaborate on your investment in digital technologies. It is obvious that you do not simply use digital technology as an architectural tool, but that new technology constitutes an integral component of your understanding of our environment. It would also be very interesting if you could characterize your architectural approach in comparison with that of each other. Although based on and derived from a somewhat similar background, the outcome of your work and of the work of your two student groups is very different – ranging from the 'traditional' architectural model to virtual and multimedia installations.

HANI RASHID: Greg and I both work on very different sides of a similar set of equations and this is one of the intriguing aspects of the outcome that we have come to see at the US Pavilion. It seems from our different approaches toward digital technologies that we have been completing the equation. Some of the perceived deficiencies in my approach, I suppose, Greg seems to take up, the corollary being true as well. That is something I appreciate in his approach to the problem of working within the digital realm. The contrasts are explicitly mapped and made manifest in the pavilion, which is very important in a period of radical shifts. I think that the students have also come to appreciate the similarities and contrasts between these two distinct approaches. This is something that is not readily available in a typical institutional setting such as Columbia or UCLA, despite the great diversity in pedagogical approaches within these settings. Greg and I have taught next to each other for years, but this kind of magnifying glass on our approaches is particular to this situation, to being on a world stage.

GREG LYNN: Although the two installations cover a pretty full spectrum, what is interesting is what we don't bother to address. For instance, it is not interesting to focus on the use of digital technologies for office automation. Most offices in the world are using CAD software to automate their office's drafting and today no one makes a big deal out of that. No one would walk into the US Pavilion and say 'They are all drawing on Autocad, this is just about digital technologies.' Similarly, they would not say 'These are fly-through animations, this is all about digital technologies.' Today both digital simulation and automation are an integral part of architectural design and production that have been digested in a very unacknowledged way. Many people are saying that this exhibition is not about architecture but about digital technology and form, but that is just because today architects are not willing to accept the role the computer plays beyond being just a tool. I am certain that in a few years this will no longer be the case and this exhibition will look like most architects' offices.

HOLLEIN: Looking beyond the tool aspect of it, what are the cultural, technical or social changes which digital technologies are bringing about that have an effect on architecture?

LYNN: This is more about Hani's work but there are components of it in both my work and the students' work. For 2000 years or more, architects have worked in a virtual world where they make abstract drawings of spaces. The emergence of digital media spaces introduces a new field with new design issues that architects are better equipped to solve than many other designers, because virtuality has been our field since we stopped building and started drawing. The computer also introduces a new aesthetic vocabulary of curves based on calculus equations. Although we have been using calculus to analyze form in the design process we have never had a tool that allows us to intuitively design using the logical curves of calculus equations.

RASHID: What is interesting about this situation is that it makes us question our approaches and positions within architectural discourse and practice. Somebody asked me in an interview earlier today about the organic in architecture and its newfound relevancy. Throughout this century, truly radical, inspired, and intriguing works, have always confronted the struggle or striving towards a kind of perfection that is perhaps, one could say, already present in nature. Computers have in effect given us critical and highly potent tools that prompt us to once again ask some fundamental questions in this regard. What does it mean to strive to that moment in an architectural work where one is close to the perfection that surrounds us?

Therefore, the computer and digital technologies effectively become extensions of both our mind and hand. I was also asked about sketching in that same interview and what relevancy the sketch has in respect to new digital technologies and tools. In the hands of my students these digital tools have made new types of sketches possible, obviously very different than the sketches we have known, nevertheless extensions of the mind to the hand. These digital 'sketches' incite a thoroughness and absolute complexity in the transfer of ideas to manifestation in a way we never had before. So in the longer history of architecture, I believe one won't be referring to the digital, rather references will be made in regard to the ongoing story of the radical. The work in the pavilion makes it very clear that it is part of a lineage, but at the same time, it is a definitive break from tradition because of these new tools. This has invariably reinvigorated architectural discourse.

HOLLEIN: I would like us to turn our attention towards the issues of teaching and research taking place within a university context. What is the attraction of academia for architects and where are the direct bridges between profession and pedagogy?

LYNN: A lot of it has to do with just how unforgiving the design and construction industry is. For a certain type of architect there is an expectation that you are going to do something cutting edge, new, groundbreaking, and original. Combined with that is an expectation that you are going to produce a design on a very tight schedule, with a fixed budget, and with many constraints. That is just the nature of architecture right now: there is a lot of interest in it, but from a very ruthless set of people who are not interested in conducting an experiment, while they do demand and experimental building. This situation has generated the possibility for a more adventurous kind of work professionally, but the inability to come up with the machinery in an office to keep doing something new. This has made the academy and its intellectual, technical, and creative resources very important. At a university, with the time, focus, and resources, you can conduct research and innovation and then have it spin off into a commercial practice. Very soon thereafter, you can bring the information about commercial practice back to the students to train them as the next generation of architects. This cycle has recently accelerated and has become a necessary network for architects like Hani and me.

HOLLEIN: Does this mean that there is a mutual benefit for both sides?

LYNN: In a certain way everybody is exploiting each other's information on a shorter cycle. Today's students are not going to universities to study with masters, often they are there to learn the latest industry tricks and then go out and see if they can get them into the field quickly. This has happened at Columbia over the last decade where the most successful recent graduates have set up their own offices where research from the university gets applied to built projects of their own and they bypass working in senior architects' offices. This means that they can make an immediate contribution to the field independently but the profession suffers from their absence from large-scale projects. You can't run a whole profession on this model but there are certain universities that are able to do so.

RASHID: One of the problems with architectural pedagogy today is the implicit and somewhat misunderstood union between the profession and the academy. The idea that students could be directed toward the practice at the expense of learning theory and experimentation is something I have questioned for some time. Greg makes it sound as if these students are ready to go into the trenches, the work force, and thrive – I'm not sure. Of course it is our hope that they will. However, I am also interested in their ability to perhaps form new types of polemical practices, some of which may not resemble practice as we know it today. The truth is that practice is still in many ways dictated by a kind of corporate methodology in which style and for-mula drive most decisions. I basically structured this situation here at the Biennale as I always have in all of my years of teaching, as a kind of research studio meshed with a micro-office situation. In my own architectural practice, Asymptote, this has had a kind of reverse effect: the practice actually spawned from discoveries I made at the academy. It became evident to me that real clients existed with real needs concerning both actual and virtual architectures, coupled with a larger definition of 'architecture' inclusive of everything from branding to physical facilities and digital environments. This demanded a new kind of approach where a great deal of tasks needed to be handled in proficient and innovative ways. This is beyond the standards of what is normally defined as professional practice, and it has prompted us to refor-mulate what it means to be an architect today, to be engaged in the totality of archi-tectural production as opposed to a singular approach of building buildings.

HOLLEIN: Both of you got involved very early on in institutional teaching. Was that turn in your career path, in your definition as an architect, a conscious decision or did it come out of constraints or sudden opportunities?

RASHID: I was a recently minted twenty-seven-year-old architect, who was struggling, as all graduates do, to establish myself, both as an architect and an individual. I needed to make a living and find a way to continue my research and establish a body of work. After completing my degrees in the US, I attempted to work in Europe where I thought there was a richer intellectual environment. I soon discovered that a young architect could not move through the entrenched European establishment. In Europe, you become an assistant to someone and it takes years before you reach a professorial position. I believe this to be an impediment to the formation of new and provocative ideas. One of the important aspects about the US Pavilion is that it makes explicit the importance of the role that young architects play, particularly at certain universities like Columbia and UCLA where research is encouraged and nurtured. I was a full-fledged professor by the time I was twenty-eight, working with my own students – some of whom were the same age or older than I was. Twelve years later I am already able to look back on a great deal of work and research. This I believe is an important place for an architect to be at forty.

HOLLEIN: Greg, at this moment you are teaching simultaneously at four different universities – ETH, UCLA, Columbia and Yale. This is not only an impressive list but also defines your understanding of the role of an architect and the amount of time you can spend on your own office work. Is this continued and probably even intensified interest in academia, solely or at least to a large part research driven?

LYNN: In addition to the resources for experimentation that a university provides, I began teaching because I wanted to write a book that would articulate the focus of my work and make my design practice. I thought that teaching was a place to test design technique and theory on these terms, to see if my work was transmittable. This is still what my teaching produces: academic research. A few years ago I started logging how I spent my time professionally on a daily basis and I realized that I spent roughly one third of my time teaching. Between the four schools you mentioned, I still spend a little less than one third of my time teaching, but now I am teaching in a more focused way. At the two schools where I regularly teach – the ETH Zürich and UCLA – I do not teach undirected studios but always tie together research in theory, technology and design through linked courses with students who are in my courses over a couple of years and whose academic careers I can follow.

RASHID: That is befitting to another situation worth noting which is the flip side of being young and attaining a teaching position. The irony is that once you finally get to a level where you have established yourself academically, you effectively don't need the teaching 'job' anymore – which is essentially when ones practice begins to take root. At that point, given the current tenure procedures and protocols, the schools often have no way of holding on to some of these teachers. Unfortunately, tenure review committees don't necessarily always look to practice as one of their important criteria. Greg mentioned the word 'visiting,' and that seems to be a general problem with academia today. One ends up participating as a perpetual visitor, which intrinsically encourages untimely departures. There is nothing in place that expresses the need for continued high level research in architectural education and one has to devise a strategy to bypass the typical tenure path. Perhaps we have to locate and develop another forum as a sort of hybrid between the office and the school. Some of us do it subversively within the institutions and get away with it. Greg has to do it in a number of places simultaneously and that is an interesting method because, sooner or later, you are found out.

HOLLEIN: As for our program at the US Pavilion in Venice and how the concept of doing an architectural workshop played out, what do you think the pavilion stands for in regard to the students?

RASHID: The work in the pavilion articulates two conditions: primarily that the students have come to realize just how much power they actually hold because they are fluent and proficient with their medium. And secondly they are aware that their research and capabilities empowers them. Ultimately they are the ones peering into the future of the profession. The pavilion doesn't just show the future of the institution or pedagogy, it also gives us a glimpse into practice today, as something in the process of mutating and forming.

HOLLEIN: The motivation and pressure for your students who took part in this must have been quite intense.

LYNN: The amazing thing was that the students were able to get everything produced, shipped across the Atlantic, installed, and in place with few hitches. Architecture indulges a lack of respect for time that we teach our students in school. What was very refreshing for me was that by putting the students in this situation they worked in a professional way and achieved more than I ever expected in 10 weeks. I constantly said to them that I wasn't on exhibition, they were. It immediately mobilized them and empowered them with a certain level of confidence, maturity, and responsibility that they wouldn't have had otherwise. I have a suspicion that some of these students will be making a significant contribution to the field ten years out because they have had this opportunity and were given this responsibility.

HOLLEIN: The whole idea of the US Pavilion program was not only to present an exhibition and a workshop to the public but also to use the Biennale as a platform and to give something back to the students who participate in it – in as much as they get a very intense exposure and interaction with an extremely sophisticated audience from their field.

LYNN: It allows them to take the temperature of the world of architecture. They have put their work up and now all cross-sections of humanity have been walking through and giving them their opinions. It has been a tough environment for them to work in, but a great place to get feedback. They get a different kind of exposure than they would ever get at a school, because they are out of context. The work in the pavilion looks like much of the work being done at UCLA, as every school has to have a focused specialized agenda and this work is typical of what is going on at UCLA and in my courses at the ETH. Here in Venice the students get a very fresh set of comments and responses that is more indicative of contemporary architecture in its diversity.

RASHID: In my case my pedagogical method was centered on the collaboration or the formation of a community attempting to remedy a syndrome of the architectural profession, the tendency towards the heroic. I have watched these students learn to appreciate the power of a true community of thinkers, each one being individual yet working in tandem to produce some really compelling work. We all know that there is a remarkable team behind every star architect no matter how popular the 'brand' name might be. One of the reviews of the exhibition stated that these students of architecture, some as young as nineteen, accomplished a more professional and intelligent work at the Biennale than many of the established architects here. That alone is an incredible endorsement and encouragement for the forming of groups and cultures that can serve to question some very staid and problematic aspects of our field.

HOLLEIN: Will all the students become architects in the way we know it? Or will their knowledge in spatial configuration and digital technologies lead them to different or even as of yet inexistent professions outside the closer circle of architecture?

RASHID: Five years ago, I was confronted by some senior and well-respected faculty members at Columbia, around the time that Greg and I starting teaching the paperless studios. In their minds my teaching method was seen as inappropriate and strange. They were convinced that our profession would not legitimize this sort of research, that architecture was only about, or at least defined as, a study towards building design. Today the field is undoubtedly in a state of radical flux and that is evidenced not only in what Greg and I are doing, but throughout this Biennale. In this respect, I fear that the architect is becoming a strange, almost pathetic character unable to grasp the changes that are taking place. The intriguing aspect of this Biennale, especially the US Pavilion, is the fact that we have lost that kind of self-conscious approach, the need to legitimatize ourselves through mimicking building practice. There is nothing wrong with some of these students going off into other interdisciplinary areas that have yet to be categorized or defined. We just don't know what they will be doing within or without architecture, and that aspect is extremely important. Fuksas gathered together a very eclectic group of architects to drive this point home. I have heard that many artists are perplexed with this Architecture Biennale because suddenly it has made the discipline of architecture interesting again.

LYNN: I think that I could repeat many of Hani's comments about expanding the field. What is linked to these comments is that for the students who decide to stay in architecture, the field will have expanded their available resources too. For example, we had to order a few hundred church pews and we found five suppliers with hundreds of different pews. We asked each of them about the possibility of customized panels and they all said we should call a fabricator in Arkansas. It turns out that all church pews in America seem to be manufactured at this one place in Arkansas where they have a mill much like the mill in this pavilion. You send them Adobe Illustrator files and they cut pews for you. I realized that every part of the construction industry is already doing what we have been promising you could do. All we had to do was take just one step outside of our little territory to find out there are all these resources that change the way we design buildings. These resources are often already in place and all we have to do is educate ourselves to use these capabilities creatively as designers. I think that these students are going to look around and say, 'How can I redefine my role as an architect?' and they are also going to say, 'How can I do a different kind of architecture by taking a step out into these other fields and bringing new techniques back to architecture?' I think it really works two ways: it expands the field and also enriches the field.

This interview took place in Venice in July 2000, during the final days of the workshop at the US Pavilion.

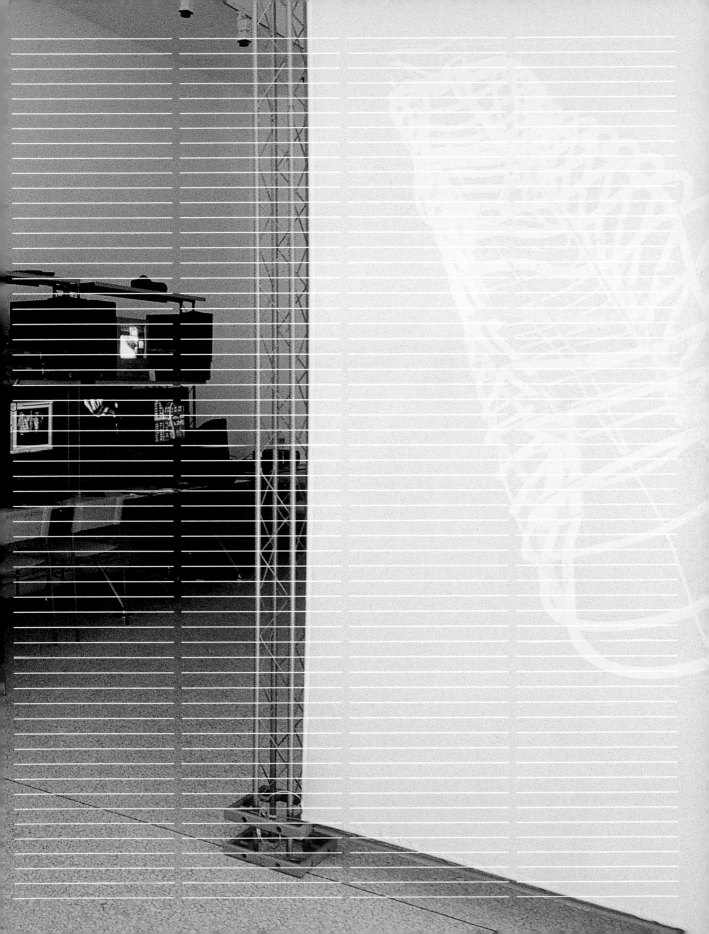

HANI RASH

PROLOGUE

HANI RASHID

The work carried out by Asymptote is a reflection of its commitment to speculative investigations and research, as well as its belief that new possibilities for architecture can be found in the exploration of spatiality within the unique conditions of our contemporary cultural context. Each project carried out at the US pavilion embodied a thematic that not only referenced ideas related to conventional architectural programs, but also sought to question what constitutes and comprises our understanding of spatiality and architecture today. Three separate installation works were enacted in the pavilion over a period of several months. The laboratory nature of the work was intentional in its attempt to avoid the prosaic and normative architectural exhibition, in order to bring both theoretical and practical issues to the surface. The three themes that were studied included the body and its dismantling through electronic media, the Internet and its impact on contemporary urbanism, and the airport as a surrogate pervasive urbanity. With the advent of computing and new forms of digital representation, entirely new forms of architectural experimentation and practices have emerged. The Columbia research laboratory environment at the 2000 Venice Biennale and the modus operandi of Asymptote are similar in their mutual aspiration to merge the 'making' and 'theorizing' of architecture.

The first of the three Venice experiments was Broadcast Architecture, a study of the implications and ramifications of the body-space dialectic we inhabit today vis-à-vis electronic mediation, televisual spectacle and real-time inhabitation of the electro-sphere. If we comprehend the world today to be one of fluctuating and mediated circumstance, whether through constant surveillance, instant replays or real-time event structures, then the body is very much implicated by virtue of either its presence or, more profoundly, its absence. The body as we understand it today transforms and mutates within this space of image transfer. This research and subsequent installation of Broadcast Architecture is an attempt to substantiate and explore this thesis. The four-dimensional data culled from the complex enactment of a gymnast's movements through space, enabled the formulation of a physical structure and enclosure. This precise mapping of the body's choreographed trajectory made plastic its spatial and temporal displacement. The resulting architectural entity allows the viewer, or perhaps more correctly, the participant, to occupy the space vicariously. The resulting one to one scaled construction, a precise multidimensional 'trace' of the gymnast's actions, allows for the projection of one's own body into the physical assembly and consequently the mediated counterpart of the installation.

The DataFlux environment continued to elaborate on the themes of real and virtual counterparts. It was based on the assumption that as we further develop information technologies, virtual interfaces, datascapes, and the like we are in effect probing further into potential new territories for spatial research and by extension architecture. The DataFlux environment, occupying much of the second gallery in the US pavilion, formed a structure that was ambiguously situated between that of a large-scale physical construction and an ephemeral, video based environment. The use of a technology called LiveWire was a key element. LiveWire consists essentially of a strand of material that allows light to be transmitted through it and from it. A large, three-dimensional 'form' constructed from this material created the 'semblance' of a physical enclosure, as though a wire frame structure had literally been liberated from the confines of the computer screen. The simultaneous video projection of feedback loops, resulting from the digital recording of the actual structure and its wire frame proxy, created a doubly 'ambiguous' spatiality. The juxtaposition of these two 'data' spaces, the physical rendition of the virtual and virtualized space of the physical, formed a constantly fluctuating territory. The DataFlux environment is an architectural space, continually transformed and resituated by the input of data and information flows that are merged with the physical entity.

The influence of aspects flow on architecture is limited not only to the realm of information and the space of the computer. This is the area of exploration in AirPort Urbanism, the third installation at the Biennale. Cities have historically evolved around trade routes and transportation nodes, including waterways, highways, and rail lines. The future of cities and the ways of corporate culture are inextricably linked. In today's continually changing global corporate culture we are seeing the evolution of city space occurring in close proximity with 'if not wedded to' new airport planning. Today the airport is a surrogate city-space equipped with all of the attributes of urbanism yet at the same time hygienically insulated and controlled. In response to the remarkable ease of global movement and a modern nomadic culture engendered by multinational corporations and air travel, a new urbanism is emerging in the hybridized condition of the airport. Schiphol in Amsterdam and Heathrow in London are examples of highly engineered spaces, not only for air traffic but also for shopping, business and entertainment. The advent of digital technologies has spawned in most business sectors two seemingly contradictory trends: long-distance communication by sophisticated electronic means, and a vast increase in travel and the need for face-to-face meetings. As businesses merge and grow around the globe, airports have attempted to keep pace by offering executive business areas, lounges, places of worship, and a plethora of other features that at one time only real city space might have provided. As airports transform into places that people not only simply pass through but instead inhabit and make use of in a number of ways, possibilities arise for new forms and new programs to be born from these spaces of flow.

The conceptual territories that were explored in the 'laboratory' of the Venice Biennale have also been the subject of much of Asymptote's recent work. Recognizing for instance that the realm of the virtual and architecture based in the physical world are not necessarily mutually exclusive, the work of Asymptote investigates and explores how one can affect and influence the other. Not unlike the Venice Biennale Laboratory projects, Asymptote's architectural forays often result in a mutating or fluctuating spatiality. The merging of physical and virtual space has been consistently explored through several installations and theoretical projects. The I-Scape studies produced by Asymptote are meditations on the meaning of information when translated to form and a revised understanding of what now constitutes spatiality. The computer and the arsenal of digital implements it has spawned have impacted all aspects of representation. The fluid and transforming I-Scape morphs revealed potential architectures that were neither appliance nor building but rather continuous and fluid tracings of fleeting spatial provocations. They fetishize mutation, distortion, and delirium, forming uncanny spaces fused with image. The dynamically generated forms are both surface and volume, following in the tradition of the works of Frederick Kiesler, Hermann Finsterlin, Andrea Bloc, and other seekers of endless space. The choreographed assemblies meander through channels of possibility and familiarity, arriving by chance at unforeseen assemblies. They are at one moment body, the next object, then metal, then plastic, at once a complex geometry and an absolute flatness. The I-Scape series underscores the inherent possibilities that data space through the medium of architecture can transcend mere numeric translation into plastic form.

The Flux installations exhibited by Asymptote from 1999 to 2002 furthered the I-Scape research through discreet experiments in digitally augmented environments where each physical construct was coupled with data streams and feeds. In Flux 1.0, constructed as part of the CAPP street artist in residency program at the California College of Art, the data feeds were projected onto a large constructed 'artifact' creating surface deformations and distortions. The accurate mapping of a three dimensional computer generated model onto an exact replica built as a physical entity produced the effect of the object being transformed and manipulated by data input. These 'distortions' were triggered by surface-embedded sensors, sensitive to movement and proximity to the object. Flux 2.0, installed outdoors at the Venice Biennale, measured eighteen meters in length and two stories in height. The form and structure, a combination of steel frame and pneumatic volume, produced a tangible oscillation between the physical exterior and the fluid continuously reconfigured state of its interior. The installation contained two 180-degree Internet cameras each set into circular rotating mirrors. These two large disk mirrors circumscribed the interior volume and were operable by way of central pivots on their main axis. Through the quasi-transparency of the rotating two-way mirrors the interior space was perceived as being in a constant state of change and reassembly. On the Internet a corresponding spatiality could be accessed and navigated by virtue of the 180 degree cameras. The combination of the manipulation of the real space by individuals physically occupying the installation and the select views captured from the webcams by Internet visitors could produce up to 1.6 million spatial variations over a period of five months. This resulting documentation describes not an architecture of stability, but one in a perpetual state of transformation, continually reconfiguring its interior spatiality as well as its relationship with its exterior surroundings.

In contrast to the Flux project, the Guggenheim Virtual Museum (GVM) is solely accessible through the Internet . With no means of physical occupancy, it takes its impetus from the notion that the body can operate in the Internet in a state of dissolution and a proxy body can be thought to displace 'space.' The fluctuating architecture of the GVM attempts to reconcile the dialectic between real and virtual, inevitably pointing the way to an architecture of convergence. The Guggenheim's physical museum, designed by Frank Lloyd Wright, comprises a spiral ramp where physical movement works in tandem with perception and experience. Today, through experimenting with virtual realities and other 'representational' technologies, we are able to theorize this space and push the parameters further. The GVM was an ideal program for confronting this history of movement and perception, and pushing the equation into mutation, flow and flux. Here, simultaneous viewing and participation are possible by a global audience via the Internet. The tectonics and formations that emerge as 'architectural' assemblies celebrate and make evident a fusion of information space, the viewing and interacting with art and the production of a fluid ever changing architectural object.

The merging of the realms of the tangible and the virtual was also explored by Asymptote in two projects for the New York Stock Exchange. First the design of the

NYSE Virtual Trading Floor (3DTF) as a reinterpretation and transformation of the existing physical trading environment set against the flows and inputs of data. The resulting virtual environment was initially developed as a wire frame model that corresponded to the 'real' trading floor. The architectural idealization needed to provide for constant shifts in scale, enhanced levels of detail, and the insertion of numerous other kinetic virtual objects. The 3DTF project took full advantage of opportunities in virtual space to manipulate spatial and temporal dimensions and provide a visual as well as spatial corollary to the actual trading environment. The 3DTF allows one to occupy several virtual spaces, scales, and points of view simultaneously. Captured events can also be instantly replayed alongside real-time events, and the user is able to compress, stretch, distort, or overlap these as required. The importance of the temporal dimension is apparent when the relationship between financial 'events' and media news reporting is made evident. Here cause-and-effect is made transparent and comprehensible as a spatial change. The project posed an interesting opportunity to reconsider the 'reality' of the actual trading floor. Asymptote's 3DTF, although virtual and not intended to be constructed outside of a computer environment, is effectively a direction for future hybrid trading environments where one moves through data occupying a physical space not unlike the DataFlux environment built in Venice.

The second work completed for the New York Stock Exchange consisted of a Command Center intervention located on the historic trading floor located on Wall Street in Manhattan. The project came about as a result of the NYSE's need to update its facilities and accommodate the 3DTF virtual-reality trading floor model and interface. The Command Center was also designed to be a theater of operations for the NYSE and a crisis management post. A primary element of the architecture is a large backlit double curved surface of blue 'pixelated' glass, an element inspired by the liquid-like nature of the movement of data and virtual information across the exchange floor. This glass wall is hung from a structure comprised of columns and horizontal steel posts. These also provide support for up to sixty high-resolution, flat-screen monitors and the array of nine other screens that display the virtual trading floor. They also serve as data feeds for the flat screen displays. The effect created is one of a floating plane of plug-and-play display panels that can be tiled and synchronized into a variety of arrangements for ultimate flexibility. The architecture is conceived as a physical analog to the movement and continuous flow of data and information throughout the space of the NYSE. The curvature of the glass and accompanying double-curved work surface accommodate both the perceived movement of data and the physical gyrations of traders frenetically moving through this space over the course of the trading day. The resulting architecture was influenced less by physical surroundings than by an attempt to spatialize the flow of data and information.

Asymptote's HydraPier building recently completed in Haarlemmermeer near Schiphol Airport embodies flows of a different sort. The architecture was designed as an artificially manufactured artifice to be situated in a predominantly artificial landscape. For much of the nineteenth century, this region lay beneath five meters of water and was reclaimed as land only 150 years ago. The architecture of the pavilion itself, two inclined and liquefied metallic planes deformed to incorporate an interior volume and an exterior pool, become an architectural landscape that is a combination of natural and technological forces. One first approaches the building below a glass pool that holds water at the 5-meter level, marking the original water datum. The inclined roofs shed their water on either side of an entrance bridge located between the two water-walls. The constant pumping and controlled flow of water fuses with the wing-like structure to create reflective and fluid surfaces. From the point of view of air travelers flying above or visitors at ground level, the pavilion's uplifted liquid wing-like roof will serve to reflect the sky by day while light and projected images will emanate at night. The water that circulates over these glistening aluminum surfaces and continually replenishing the pool is visible through the glazed underside of the pool as well as through openings in the roof. The resultant spatial condition plays upon the displacement of water and through the constant play of light and reflectivity it alludes to the manipulations that were necessary to create its own context.

Both Asymptote's research and practice and the research work carried out at the US Pavilion are ultimately concerned with the reconciliation of the dialectic between virtual and real space and investigations of what constitutes convergence in terms of digital and analog procedures. The future of architecture will without a doubt be centered around notions of digitally augmented environments and mutable territories that will inevitably lead the way to new architectures.

BODY IN MEDIA SPACE

HANI RASHID

Dissolution of the physical body from Muybridge to Duchamp to Viola . . . occupancy of media-space . . . augmentation of scale, program and form . . . the body thought of instead as a delineation of data, flow and flux . . . the body as interface, as trajectory as scribe.

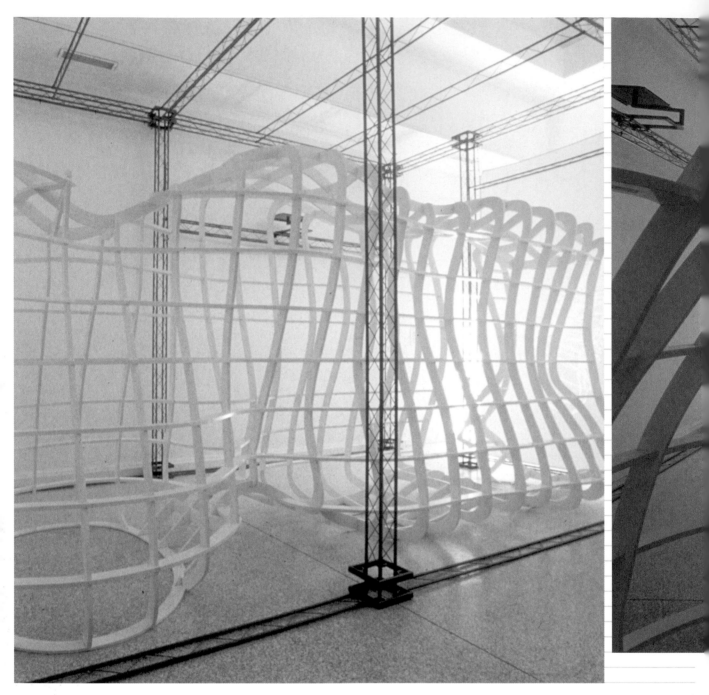

ALIAS _ _MAYA_ _ _COSMO_WORLDS_VRML_ _

Broadcast Architecture

A single gymnast's movements through space form complex geometries that are in turn broadcast back into a real space. This procedure allows for a new architecture to be formed from the notion that architectural space and form can be renegotiated by the fusion of the body and its implicit geometrical formations in movement and the displacement of space. The Broadcast Architecture installation traces a territory of ambiguity between scale, movement, time, and presence. The architectural entity is itself a preparatory work for re-broadcasting when implemented over the internet. Here it will continue to be scrutinized through notions of instant replay, rewind as well as privileged points of view, simultaneity and other key operations normally confined to the domains of media and the televised event.

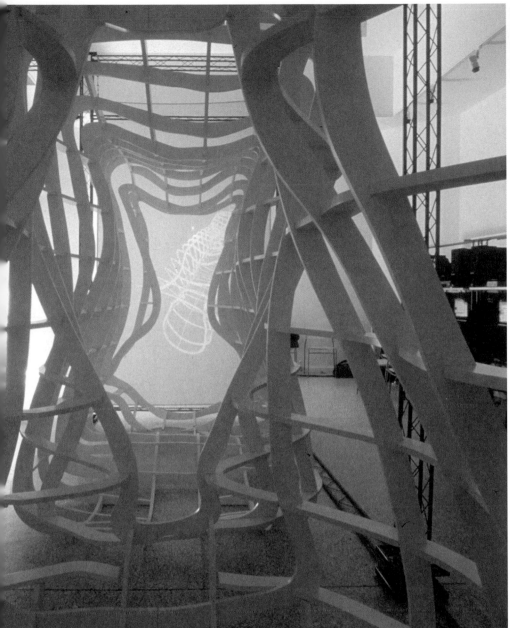

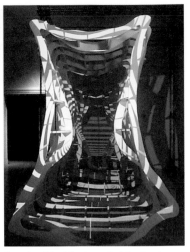

Broadcast Architecture, Architectural Laboratories, Venice Biennale, Venice, Italy (2000)
∧ Analysis of structure from computer generated animation study
< View from 'gymnasts' starting point
<< Installation, constructed by local Venetian Boat Builders, length 11m, height 2,2m, width 1,85m

DOBE_PHOTOSHOP_ _ _ADOBE_PREMIERE_ _ _M

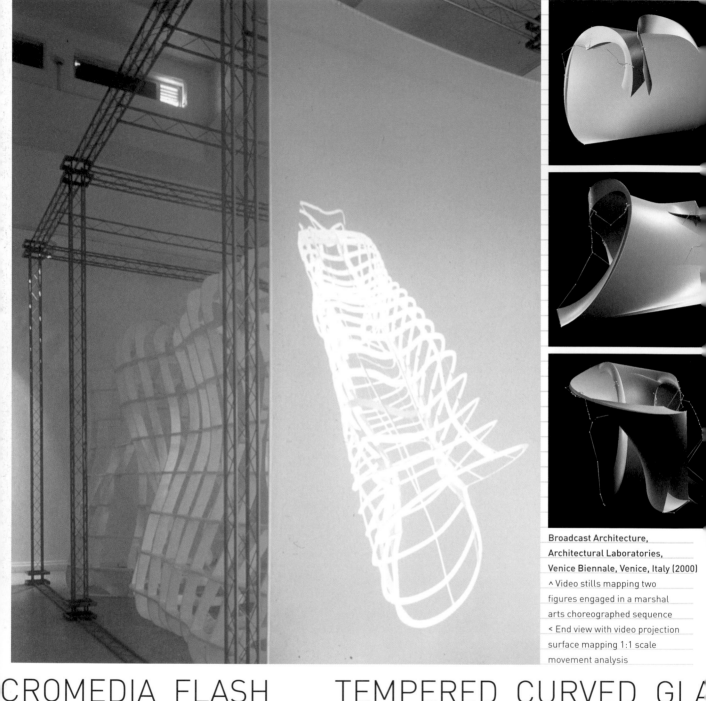

Broadcast Architecture,
Architectural Laboratories,
Venice Biennale, Venice, Italy (2000)
∧ Video stills mapping two
figures engaged in a marshal
arts choreographed sequence
< End view with video projection
surface mapping 1:1 scale
movement analysis

CROMEDIA_FLASH_ _ _TEMPERED_CURVED_GLA

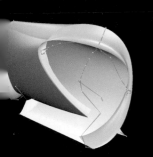

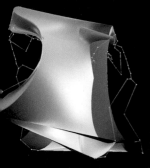

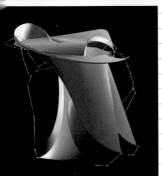

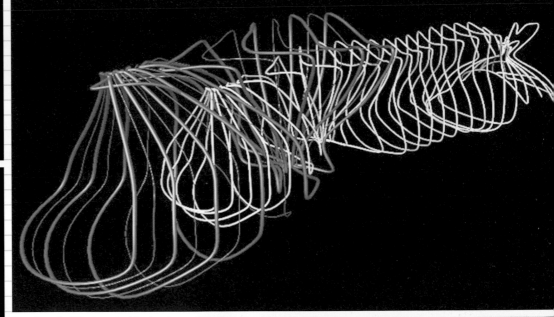

Broadcast Architecture, Architectural Laboratories, Venice Biennale, Venice, Italy (2000)

^ Video still mapping the movement of a gymnasts maneuvers through the American Pavilion, developed as a wire frame for eventual construction at 1:1

> Video still from skinning analysis film sequence

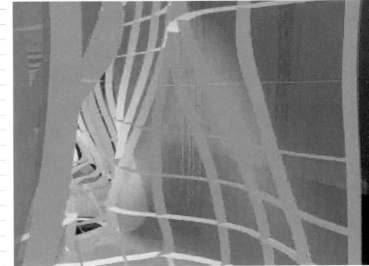

_WITH_COLOR_LAMINATE_ _ _LCD_FLAT-SCREEN

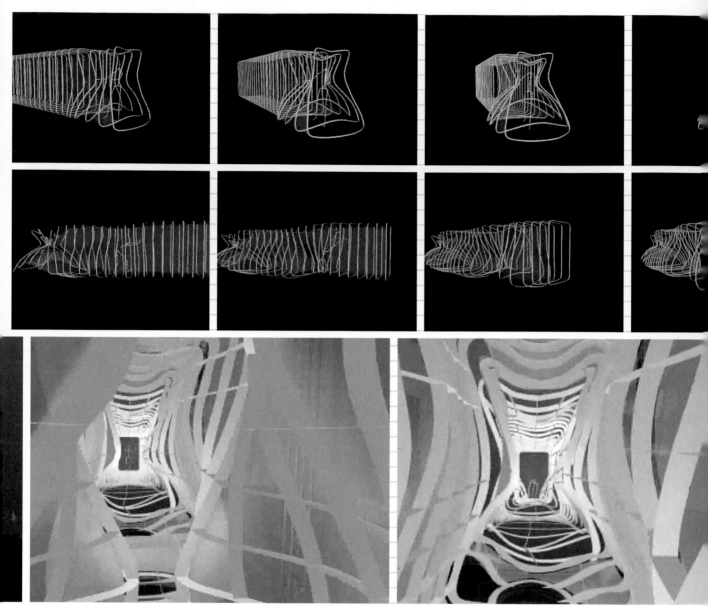

Broadcast Architecture, Architectural Laboratories, Venice Biennale, Venice, Italy (2000)
Video captures of gymnasts movements mapped into the installation proposal

MONITORS___FORMED_STEEL_STRUCTURE__

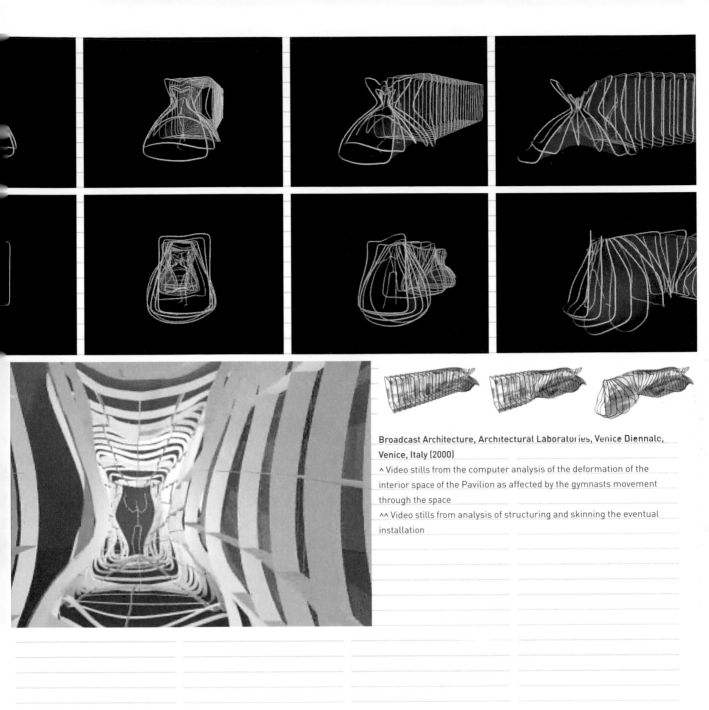

Broadcast Architecture, Architectural Laboratories, Venice Diennale, Venice, Italy (2000)
∧ Video stills from the computer analysis of the deformation of the interior space of the Pavilion as affected by the gymnasts movement through the space
∧∧ Video stills from analysis of structuring and skinning the eventual installation

OXY_FLOORING___STEEL_CABINETRY___FIBEF

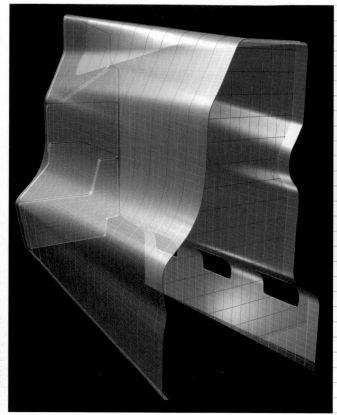

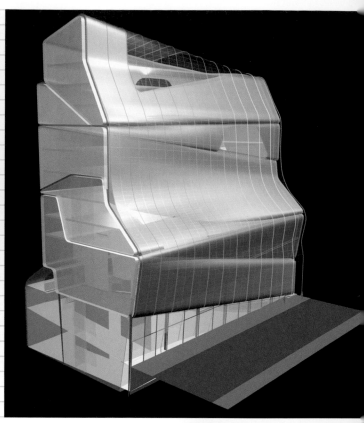

Eyebeam Museum of Art and Technology, New York, NY (2001)

^ Skinning Study for buildings exterior treatment

^> Rendering of final building proposal incorporating digital skin and manipulatable interior volumes

OPTIC_AND_COLD_CATHODE_LIGHTING___SILIC

Eyebeam Museum of Art and Technology

This proposal for a museum of digital art in Manhattan consists of an inner-block insertion that provides exhibition, delivery, auditorium, and event spaces and offices on the upper floors.

The project was developed with the idea of maximizing the galleries' usability and accessibility through 'hinging' floors and transformable interior spaces. The structure is comprised of folded pre-stressed concrete slabs and is column free.

The exterior skin is made of electronically infused glass panels capable of displaying 256 shades of gray. Through computer programming it can display large-scale moving images over the entire building skin.

Eyebeam Museum of Art and Technology, New York, NY (2001)

∧ View of main gallery interior with video surfaces and circulation ramps. View of model interior 1:200

< Structural analysis of the buildings interior utilizing a single surface incorporating slabs and walls simultaneously

_GRAPHICS_02_AND_ONYX_COMPUTERS___MU

Eyebeam Museum of Art and Technology, New York, NY (2001)
View of Streaming Gallery with video flooring. View of model interior 1:200

LTIMEDIA_VIDEO_PROJECTION_UNITS___COMPU

Eyebeam Museum of Art and Technology, New York, NY (2001)
View of ground floor and circulation to level B. View of model interior 1:200

RS___HEAT-SENSITIVE_RECEPTORS___PLASTE

Eyebeam Museum of Art and Technology, New York, NY (2001)
View of theater space and circulation ramps. View of model interior 1:200

R___LATHE___WOOD___PNEUMATIC_MEMBRA

Eyebeam Museum of Art and Technology, New York, NY (2001)
^ View of lower level 'sculpture' gallery. View of model interior 1:200
^^ View of ground floor gallery interior with lecture space engaged. View of model interior 1:200

AND_STEEL_STRUCTURE___ONE-WAY_MIRROR

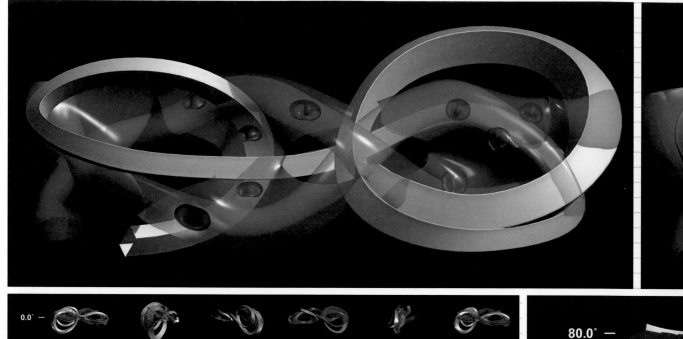

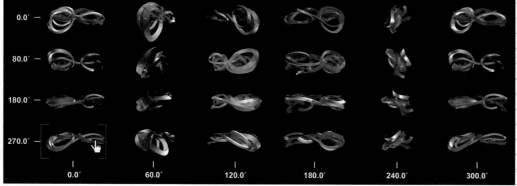

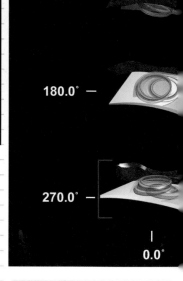

Guggenheim Virtual Museum, New York, NY/Internet (1999-2001)

∧ Gallery sequence interface

∧∧ Gallery domain articulating virtual circulation zones and artists' galleries

ED_PLEXIGLAS_DIAPHRAGMS___IPIX WEB CAME

Guggenheim Virtual Museum
The Virtual Museum is an
Internet-based museum,
housing digital and Internet art.
It encompasses a number of
virtual user experiences in the
viewing and surveying of recent
electronic acquisitions as well

as other Guggenheim Museum
content.

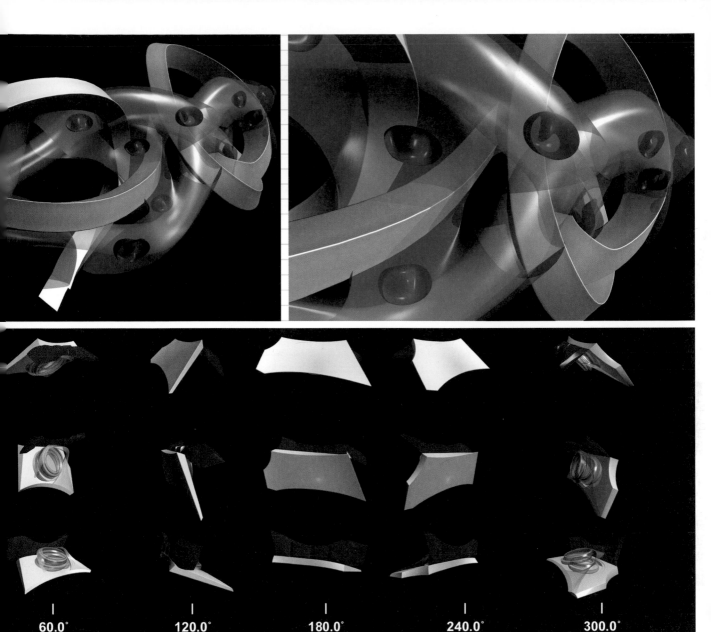

60.0°   120.0°   180.0°   240.0°   300.0°

Guggenheim Virtual Museum, New York, NY/Internet (1999-2001)

∧ 'Plaza' sequence interface study

∧∧ Gallery domain articulating virtual circulation zones and artists galleries

S _ _ _COMPUTERS_ _ _FLUORESCENT_LIGHTING

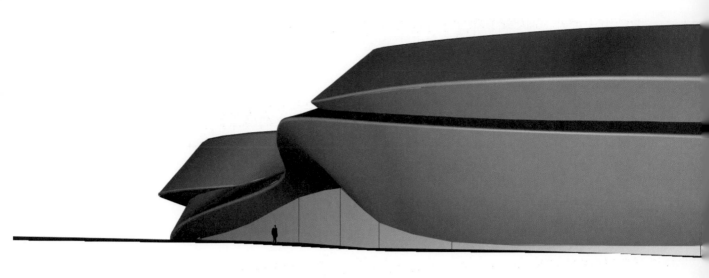

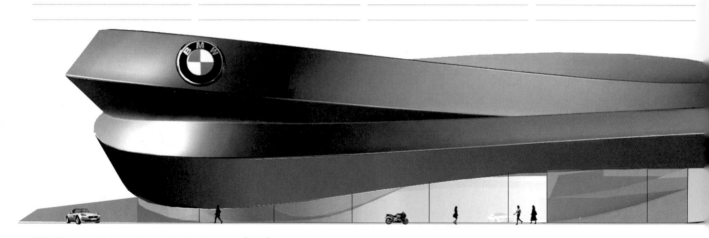

BMW Event and Delivery Center, Munich, Germany (2001)
Elevation studies

_CONCRETE_AND_WOOD_FOUNDATION_AND_FL

BMW Event and Delivery Center

This is a building designed to allow visitors and customers to experience the BMW brand through a variety of functions, ranging from virtual-reality simulation test-drives to show-casing the latest prototype models. The building is designed as a public facility where customers not only acquire their newly delivered automobiles but experience the 'brand' at many levels from product to spatial design. The tectonics of the building are predicated on the movement of vehicles and visitors through space. Cars are able to travel throughout the entire interior of the facility and are on show throughout their trajectory.

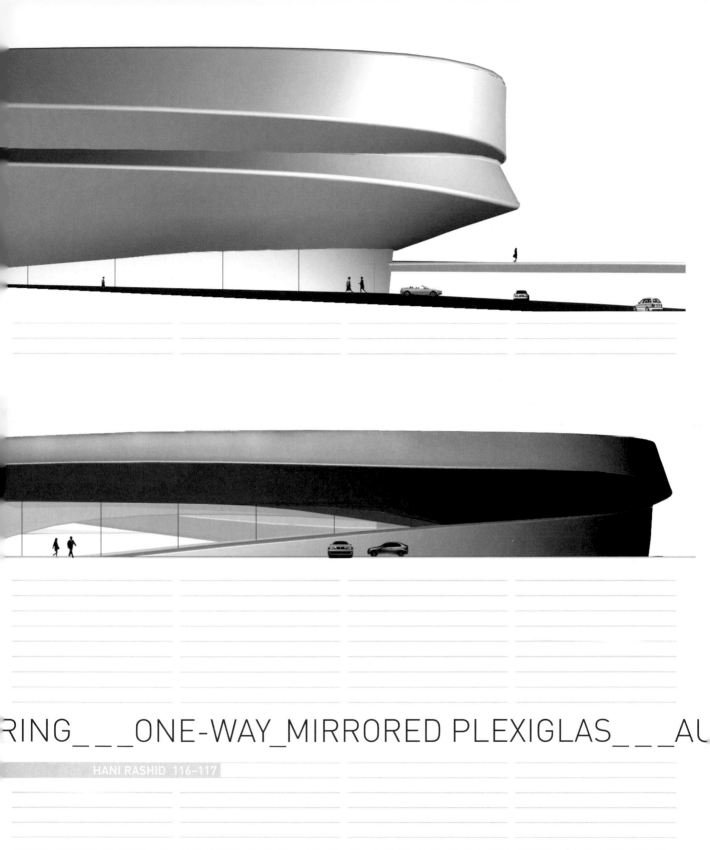

RING___ONE-WAY_MIRRORED PLEXIGLAS___AU

TO_POLES___PIXEL-VISION_LCD_MONITORS__

BMW Event and Delivery Center, Munich, Germany (2001)

^ Exterior form study

< Interior view of 'auto-delivery' theater and circulation ramps

MPUTERS___ALIAS___MAYA___COSMO_WORLD

New York Stock Exchange Advanced Trading Floor, New York, NY (1997-2000)
Views of the trading and 'staging' area. Constructed in formed steel panels, 3D curved
glass, containing 60 plasma monitors and integrated computer systems and lighting

S_VRML___ADOBE_PHOTOSHOP___ADOBE_PRE

New York Stock Exchange
This is the main operations
component of the New York
Stock Exchange's trading floor
in New York. The Command
Center houses all necessary
data displays and computer
support systems as well as

the Asymptote-designed 3DTF
Virtual Reality Environment.

New York Stock Exchange Advanced
Trading Floor, New York, NY (1997-2000)
Views of the navigation area for the
3DTF Virtual Stock Exchange

ERE___MACROMEDIA_FLASH___TEMPERED_CU

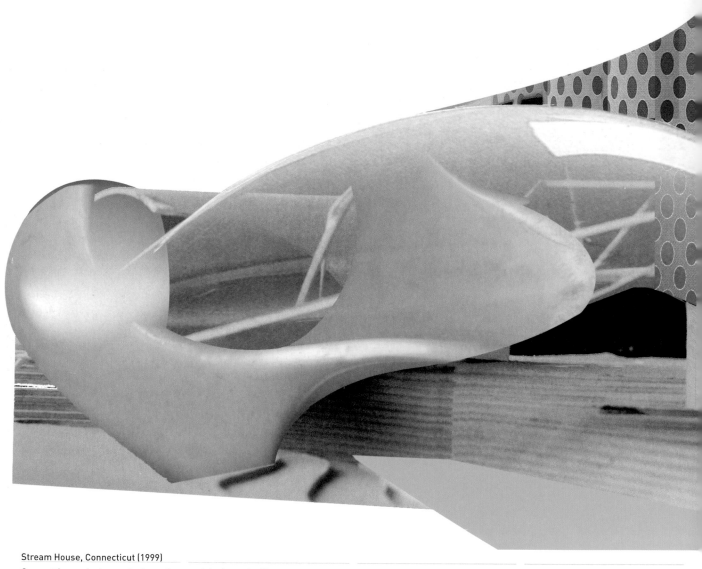

Stream House, Connecticut (1999)

Concept for a private country home for an art dealer and collector

RVED_GLASS_WITH_COLOR_LAMINATE___LCD_F

T-SCREEN_MONITORS___FORMED_STEEL_STRU

DATA-FLUX

HANI RASHID

Mapping information as architectural form . . . information space as architecture . . . information as field, tectonic, geometry and place . . . mnemonic containment . . . the experience of replay reality . . . data driven entities manipulated by presence, voice and touch . . . the experience of information as visceral . . . architectural space manipulated as multi-media.

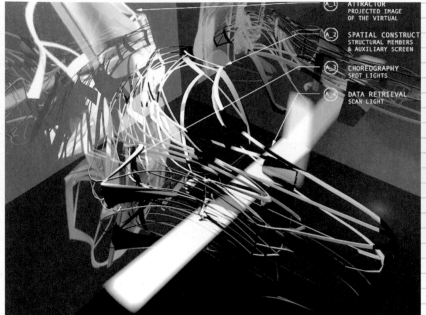

A_1 ATTRACTOR
PROJECTED IMAGE
OF THE VIRTUAL

A_2 SPATIAL CONSTRUCT
STRUCTURAL MEMBERS
& AUXILIARY SCREEN

A_3 CHOREOGRAPHY
SPOT LIGHTS

A_4 DATA RETRIEVAL
SCAN LIGHT

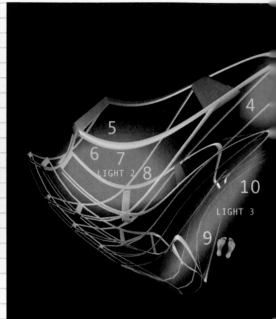

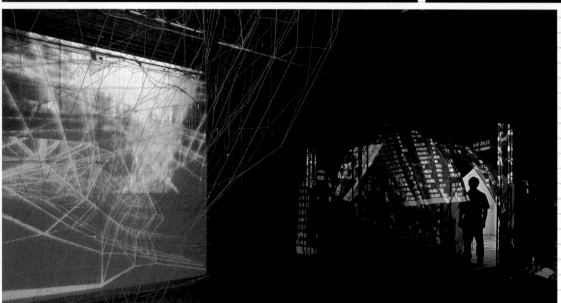

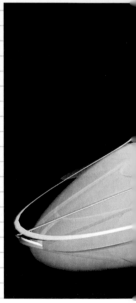

Performance Architecture, Architectural Laboratories, Venice Biennale, Venice, Italy (2000)
View of the installation at the US Pavilion

CTURE___EPOXY_FLOORING___STEEL_CABINET

Performance Architecture

An architecture constructed of lines of light implies a form and presence through the mimicry of techniques of modeling space in computer environments. The operations of modeling and design in the computer lend themselves to an ethereal manifestation of line, volume and scale. The performance apparatus structure re-enacts the procedures of manipulating computer generated data in order to construct a hybrid entity that is simultaneously a virtual projection, and a real construct. The project is online and through its internet presence it is capable of being transformed by virtue of the ambient condition in which it exists. The structure is to be read as a 'real-time' computer generated and fluctuating architecture, a space and structure in a state of perpetual performance. By virtue of live fed projections produced on site at the Pavilion the project is in constant range of development and augmentation.

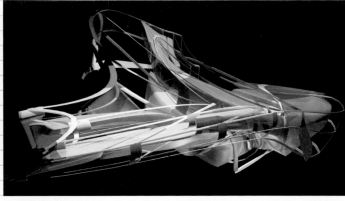

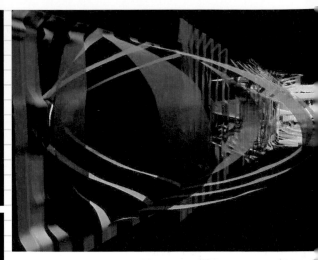

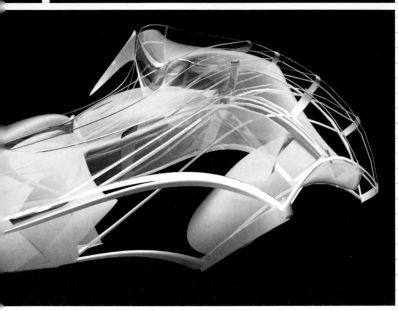

Performance Architecture, Architectural Laboratories, Venice Biennale, Venice, Italy (2000)
Various studies of the architecture of a data environment as mapped into physical space, taking into account physical movement, virtual presence, and data flows as generative structures and tectonic manipulation

___FIBER_OPTIC_AND_COLD_CATHODE_LIGHTIN

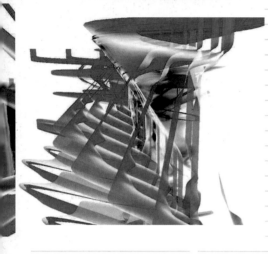

NYSE 3DTF Virtual Reality Environment, New York, NY (1997-2000)
Two views captured from the active model, computer captured stills

NYSE 3DTF

This is a large-scale, real-time information model exhibiting flows and various data-mapping capabilities for use by the operations team at the New York Stock Exchange. The virtual-reality environment allows users to monitor and correlate the stock exchange's daily trading activity and present the information within a fully interactive, multidimensional environment.

RS___MULTIMEDIA_VIDEO_PROJECTION_UNITS

NYSE 3DTF Virtual Reality Environment, New York, NY (1997-2000)

Computer captured still frame

__COMPUTERS___HEAT-SENSITIVE_RECEPTORS

_PLASTER___LATHE___WOOD___PNEUMATIC

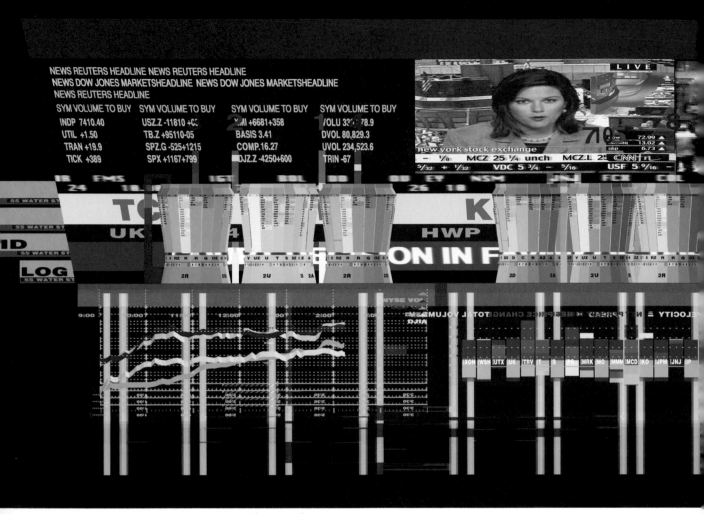

NYSE 3DTF Virtual Reality Environment, New York, NY (1997-2000)
Computer captured still frame of model elevation

MEMBRANE_AND_STEEL_STRUCTURE___ONE_

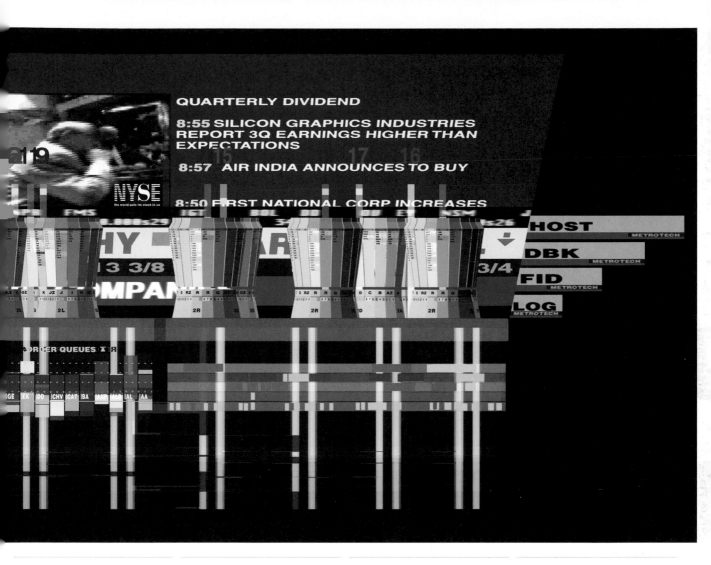

QUARTERLY DIVIDEND

8:55 SILICON GRAPHICS INDUSTRIES
REPORT 3Q EARNINGS HIGHER THAN
EXPECTATIONS

8:57 AIR INDIA ANNOUNCES TO BUY

8:50 FIRST NATIONAL CORP INCREASES

NYSE
the world puts its stock in us

HOST
DBK
FID
LOG

Y_MIRRORED_PLEXIGLAS_DIAPHRAGMS_ _ _IPIX_

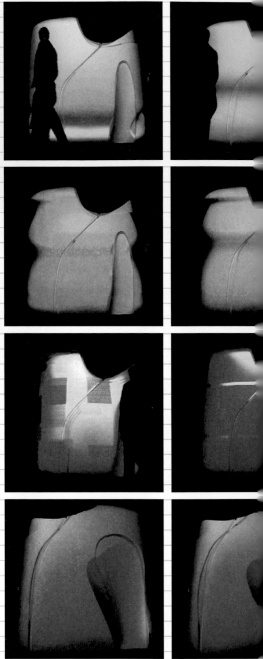

**FluxSpace1.0 Installation, CCAC
gallery, San Francisco, CA (2000)**
^ Video capture of the installation
object, constructed of wood, plaster
lathe and latex. Length 3,0m, height
3,0m, width 1,8m
> Video capture sequence of the
variations and changes in the installation's form and topological condition,
prompted by touch sensors imbedded
into the surface of the object

_WEB_CAMERAS___COMPUTERS___FLUORESC

Fluxspace 1.0 Installation
Fluxspace 1.0 is a multimedia
installation utilizing computer
and projection technologies
in tandem with a larger-scale
built artifact equipped with
touch sensors. These 'virtual
buttons' are projected onto the
surface of the object and activated by the gallery occupants.
These in turn activate a series
of video projections and sound-
scapes that alter the appearance of the artifact and create
the effect of fluctuating physical states.

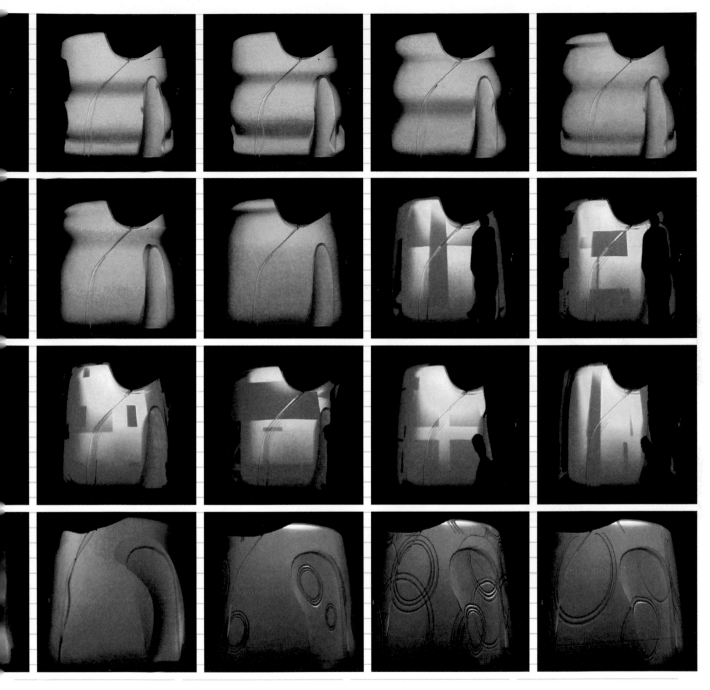

T_LIGHTING___CONCRETE_AND_WOOD_FOUND

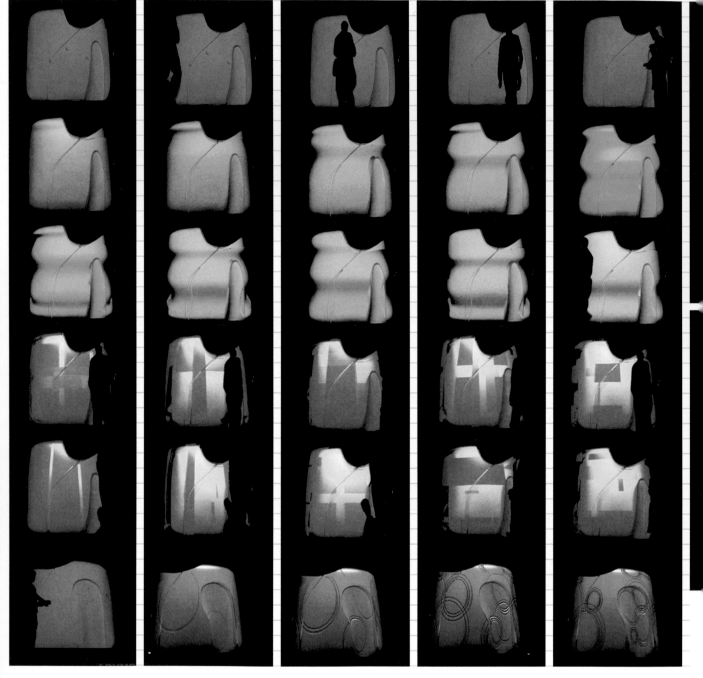

ATION_AND_FLOORING___ONE_WAY_MIRRORED

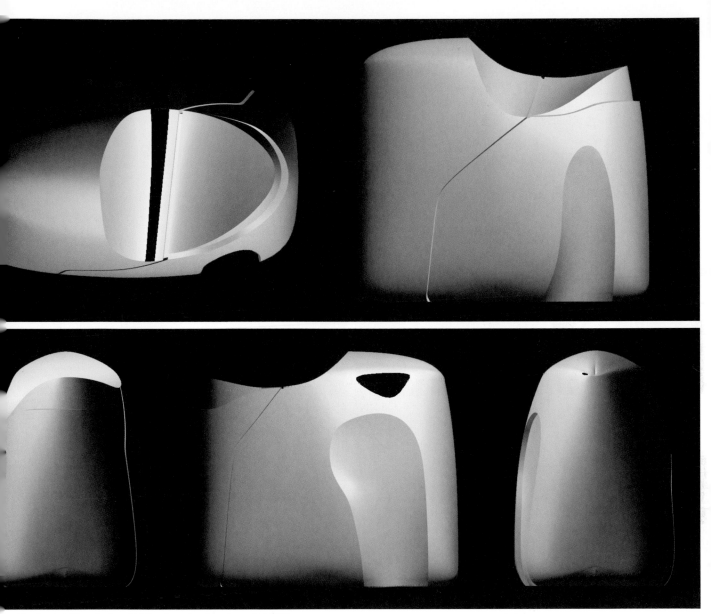

FluxSpace1.0 Installation, CCAC gallery, San Francisco, CA (2000)

∧ Computer generated studies of the 'receiver' object for construction purposes

< Video capture sequence of the variations and changes in coloration and effects

LEXIGLAS_ _ _AUTO_POLES_ _ _PIXEL_VISION_LC

HANI RASHID 136-137

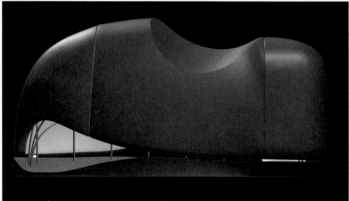
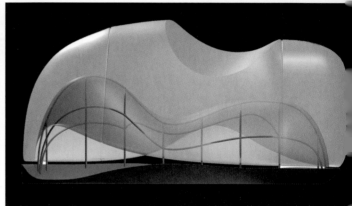

FluxSpace 2.0 Pavilion, Venice Biennale, Venice, Italy (2000)

^ Exterior and interior studies of the Pavilion

^^ Web-cam captures of the interior space

Fluxspace 2.0 Pavilion

The Fluxspace 2.0 Pavilion is a large-scale temporary inter-vention at the Venice Biennale 2000. The two-story-high, air-filled envelope was sup-ported by an elaborate steel-frame structure that formed the installation interior. Two pivoting Plexiglas diaphragms measuring 8 feet in diameter were equipped with IPIX cameras capable of recording images at thirty-second inter-vals. The resulting images of the constantly changing interior 'architectures' were published on the Internet in real time. The project produced 1.54 million distinct images of the interior volume and the distor-tions and changes that unfold-ed over the five-month duration of the Biennale.

FluxSpace 2.0 Pavilion, Venice Biennale, Venice, Italy (2000)
View of interior of the pavilion, with one way mirror, webcam, steel frame structure and pneumatic envelope. Length 15m, height 10m, width 6m

_ _ COSMO_WORLDS_VRML_ _ _ ADOBE_PHOTOSH

FluxSpace 2.0 Pavilion, Venice Biennale, Venice, Italy (2000)

> View of interior of the pavilion

OP___ADOBE_PREMIERE___MACROMEDIA_FLA

___TEMPERED_CURVED_GLASS_WITH_COLOR_L

AMINATE___LCD_FLAT_SCREEN_MONITORS___

I.Scapes Installation

The proliferation of images prompted the series of works I.Scapes. Each I.Scape is a manipulated entity using a combination of image collage, three-dimensional models, and texture maps to create ambiguous images and territories that can be read as object and field simultaneously. The installation incorporated the I.Scapes studies into morphing assemblies that were transmitted onto 24 flat-screen LCD monitors. The monitors were set into a free-standing structure constructed of one-way Plexiglas sheets that reflected and refracted the moving images within the structure's interior. The images were in constant motion produced by means of morphing

I.Scapes Installation, Frederieke Taylor-TZ Art Gallery, New York, NY (1999)

View of interior spatiality generated by 27 plasma monitors and a one way mirror structure connecting them. Length 5m, height 2,0m, width 1,6m

RMED_STEEL_STRUCTURE___EPOXY_FLOORING

software and were transmitted
into the installation's iterior.

AIRPORT URBANISM

HANI RASHID

Airports today can be thought of as infinitely extruded urbanity, that seemingly morph time and space into a single, endless structure of delirium and desire.

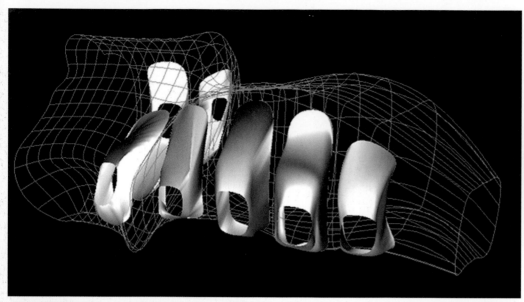

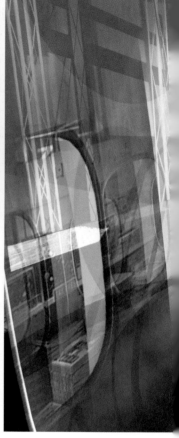

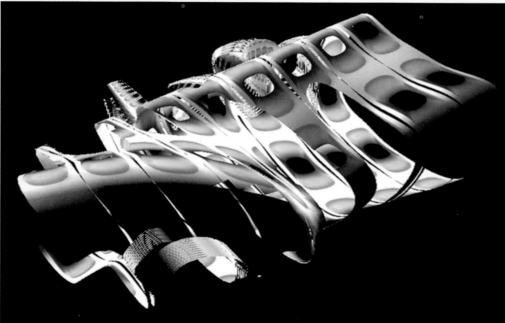

Airport Urbanism, Architectural Laboratories, Venice Biennale, Venice, Italy (2000)
Surface map studies for the fuselage construction into the US pavilion

_STEEL_CABINETRY___FIBER_OPTIC_AND_COL

Airport Urbanism

This project explored airports as surrogate urban centers that provide many of the amenities, events, and attributes of the cities which they are tethered to and reliant on. The future of city space is implicitly tied to air travel and airport infrastructure. The notion of the central business district as a place relegated solely to city centers is now becoming obsolete. Instead, new city space is beginning to prevail at airports, and to be dislodged from any one place and strewn across the globe. Airport Urbanism is a study of such a phenomenon, where the future of both airports and cities is fused as a singular initiative. This new city space is where business meetings, health clubs, recreational facilities, and even housing are developed within the space of what we traditionally called the airport.

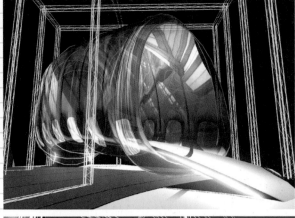

Airport Urbanism, Architectural Laboratories, Venice Biennale, Venice, Italy (2000)
∧ Study of the interior volume and structure for the fuselage construction
> Various studies for the exterior and interior of the fuselage structure for eventual
deployment in the US Pavilion

CATHODE_LIGHTING_ _ _SILICON_GRAPHICS_02_

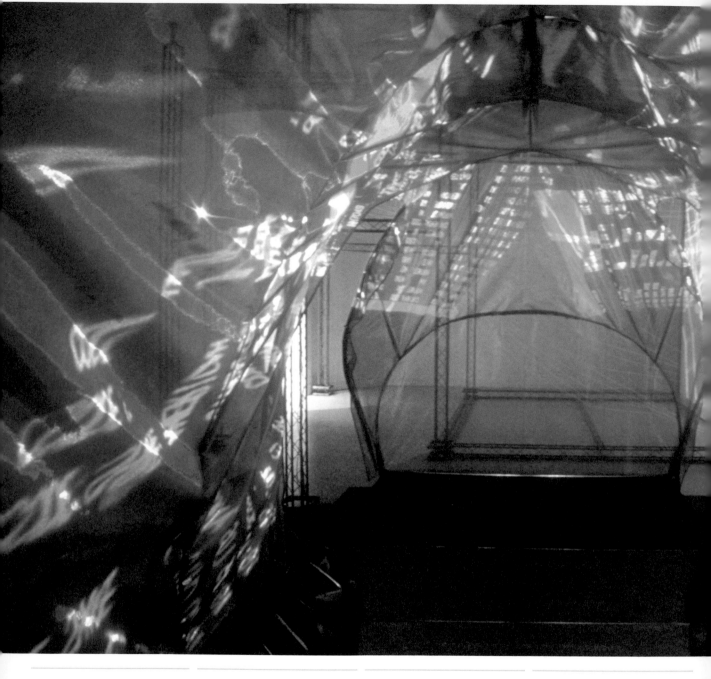

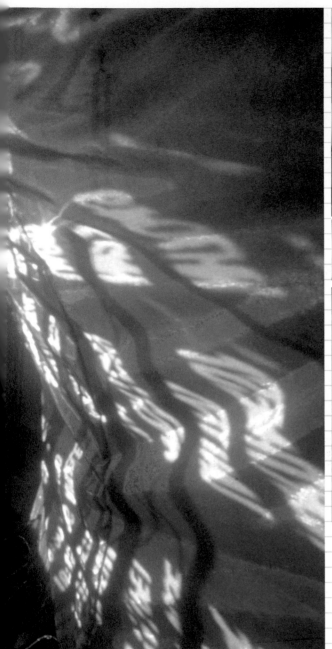

Airport Urbanism, Architectural Laboratories, Venice Biennale, Venice, Italy (2000)
^ Study for a virtual duty free environment
< Installation interior view
<< View of the fuselage structure installed into the US Pavilion, constructed of steel, metal coated scrim, interactive ramp, speakers and video projection units

ROJECTION_UNITS___COMPUTERS___HEAT-SE

AirCity (2000)
Contact zone and running track

NSITIVE_RECEPTORS___PLASTER___LATHE__

Airport Urbanism

Airports can be understood as infinitely extruded urbanisms that morph time and space in a single endless structure. Their familiarity articulates and makes explicit aspects of recognizable urban artifacts. The airport condenser is a vehicle that captures and transforms such phenomena. This allows for the exploration of augmented architecture in the forms of sound, densities and rhythms. There is both the nuance of locality set against the anonymity of place. The windows, hall, live and taped projections, sounds, and motion place the visitor in an uncanny situation, somewhere between the gangway and the duty-free zone, a non-place of movement, inhabitation and transformation.

VOOD_ _ _PNEUMATIC_MEMBRANE_AND_STEEL_

AirCity (2000)
Brand center

STRUCTURE___ONE_WAY_MIRRORED_PLEXIGLA

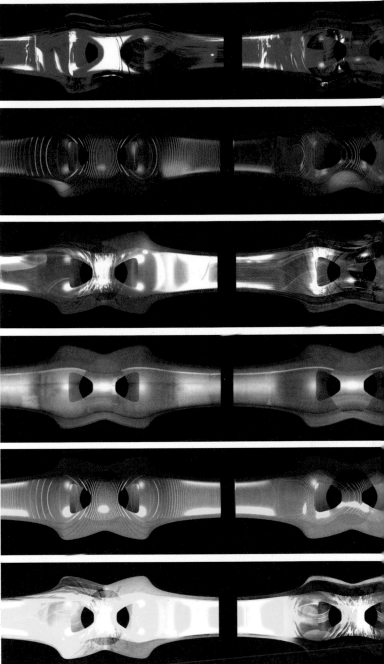

M(otion)scape

> Video still compilation of mscape object augmented
by computer generated animation sequence

DIAPHRAGMS___IPIX_WEB_CAMERAS___COMP

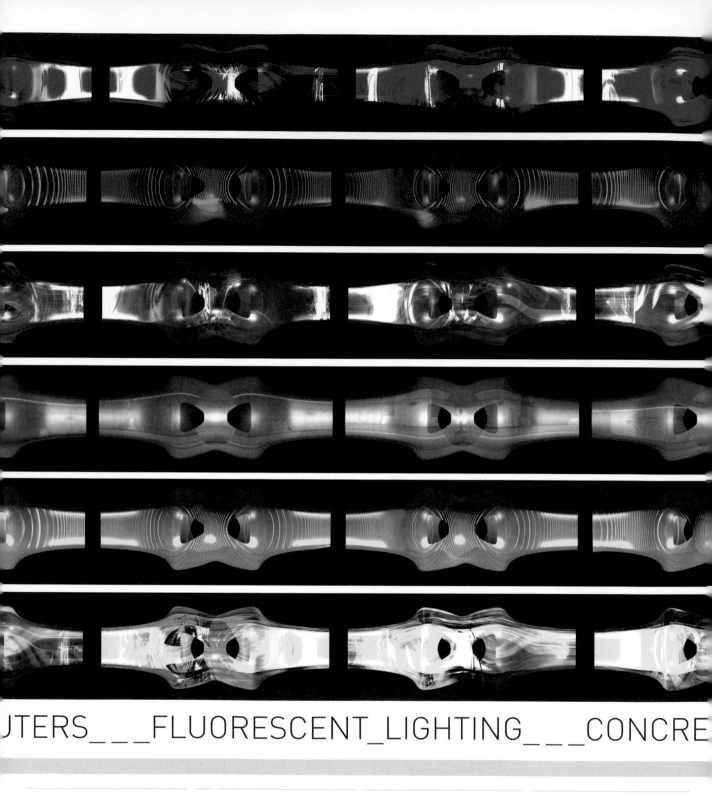

UTERS___FLUORESCENT_LIGHTING___CONCRE

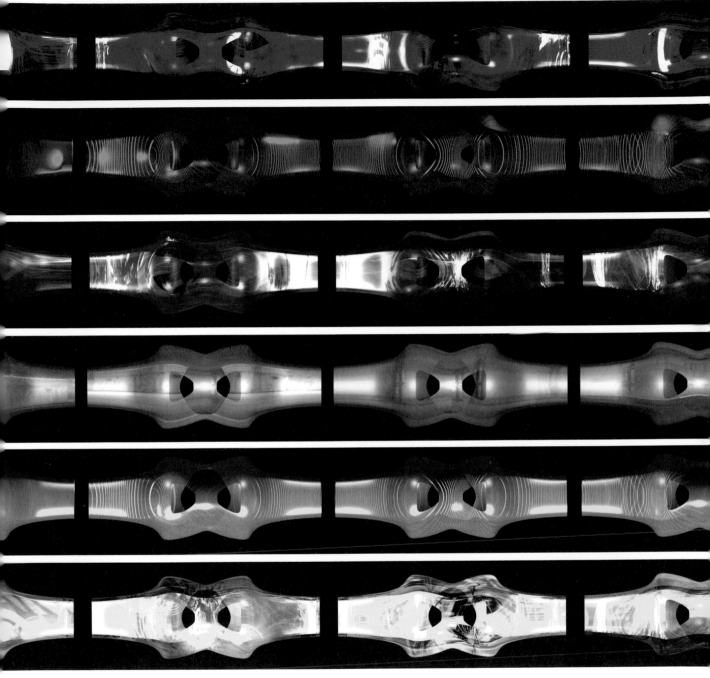

_AND_WOOD_FOUNDATION_AND_FLOORING___

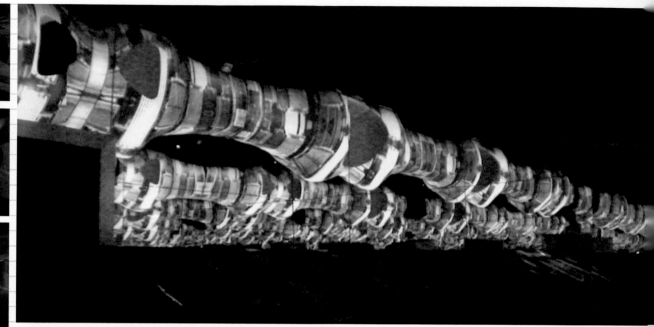

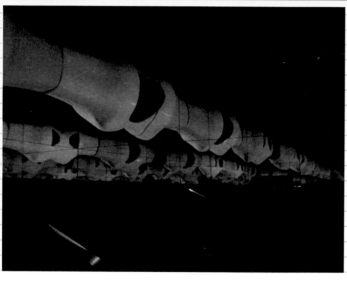

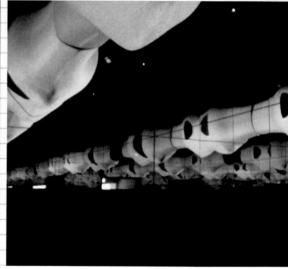

ONE_ WAY_MIRRORED_PLEXIGLAS_ _ _AUTO_POL

FluxSpace 3.0/Mscapes

This work created for Documenta XI, is an installation of an infinite environment of digital data. The content of the digital material relates to the contemporary urbanism of Hong Kong, Tokyo, New York and other global cities. The skyline of each city was abstracted into an animated image map and then sequentially projected onto a large suspended form we derived from the tectonics of a car body. In this piece, the automobile body functions as a receiver or absorber of information as it moves through the space of the city – creating 'motion scapes' (mscapes). The notational systems that result from the abstraction of the skylines were also reinterpreted as diagrams capable of 'replaying' the city as a sonic poem or soundtrack. While the texture maps reveal an apparent repetitiveness and similarity between one urban entity and another, the superimposition of the soundtracks allow for cultural inflections to be discerned.

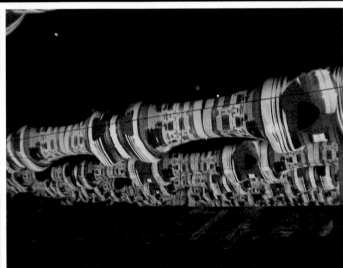

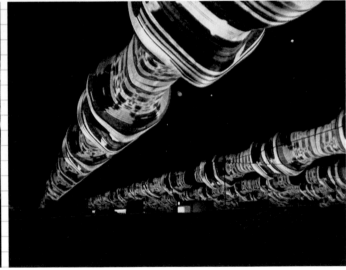

Flux 3.0/Mscapes, Documenta XI, Kassel, Germany (2002)
Various video captures of the installation work. Polystyrene formed shell structures augmented by video sequences. Length 8m, height 5m, width 4,5m

___PIXEL_VISION_LCD_MONITORS___COMPUTE

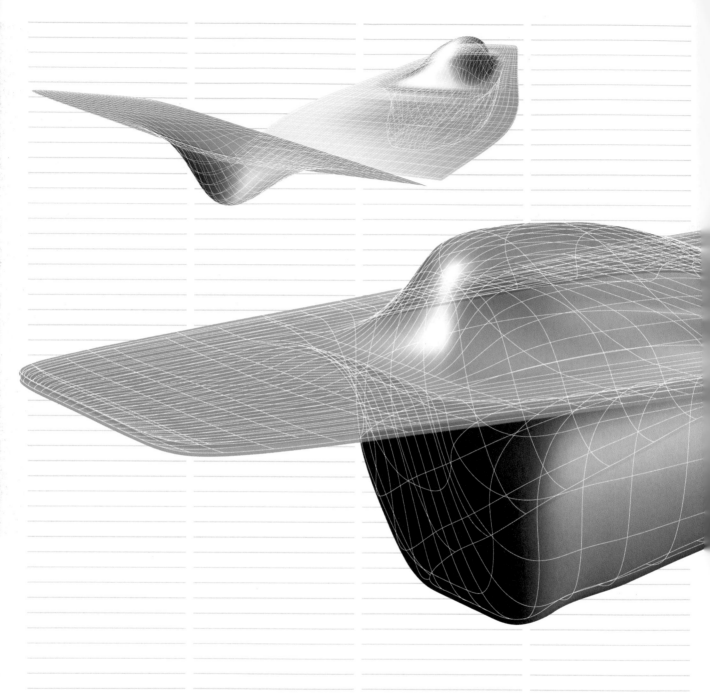

RS_ _ _ALIAS_ _ _MAYA_ _ _COSMO_WORLDS_VRM

Hydra-Pier

The Hydra-Pier is the main gateway pavilion for the Floriade festival in Haarlemmermeer. The project is sited near Schiphol Airport and commemorates both the technologies of flight and of land retrieval through the pumping of vast quantities of water. The structure is 100 meters (300 feet) long and sited on an artificial body of water and landscape. When activated, the pavilion is covered in a sheath of water that cascades over its entire envelope, forming two vertical planes of water through which people enter.

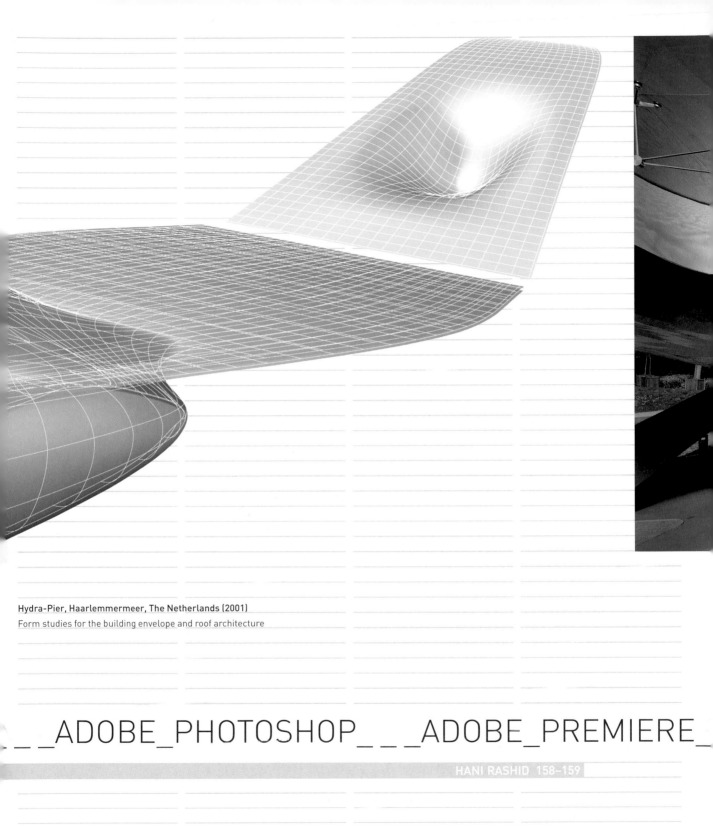

Hydra-Pier, Haarlemmermeer, The Netherlands (2001)
Form studies for the building envelope and roof architecture

_ _ _ADOBE_PHOTOSHOP_ _ _ADOBE_PREMIERE_

Hydra-Pier, Haarlemmermeer, The Netherlands (2001)

^ View from under roof structure towards the water corridor

> View of structural pier

_MACROMEDIA_FLASH___TEMPERED_CURVED

LASS_WITH_COLOR_LAMINATE___LCD_FLAT_SC

Hydra-Pier, Haarlemmermeer, The Netherlands (2001)
Exterior view

REEN_MONITORS_ _ _FORMED_STEEL_STRUCTU

_ _ _EPOXY_FLOORING_ _ _STEEL_CABINETRY_ _

Hydra-Pier, Haarlemmermeer, The Netherlands (2001)
View of structural pier

Hydra-Pier, Haarlemmermeer, The Netherlands (2001)
View of the Hydra-Pier 'vessel' with interior stair

FIBER_OPTIC_AND_COLD_CATHODE_LIGHTING_

SILICON_GRAPHICS_02_AND_ONYX_COMPUTERS

DEREGULATION

MARK C. TAYLOR

We might begin by thinking about the implications of the title of the Biennale, 'Less Aesthetics More Ethics.' There is a dialectic built into the title between less and more, on the one hand, and, on the other hand, aesthetics and ethics. It would be possible to write a history of twentieth-century architecture around the interplay between less and more. The most famous articulation of this is of course Mies' dictum 'less is more,' which has been so influential throughout the first half of this century.

'Less Aesthetics More Ethics': the relationship between aesthetics and ethics. This phrasing of the issue sets up aesthetics and ethics in more or less an oppositional relationship. What seems implied is a call for less aesthetics, which would lead to more ethics; architecture, in other words, should be less about aesthetics and more about ethics. However, this opposition or polarity between aesthetics and ethics is misleading. One way to understand a great deal of what has happened in the course of Modernism is to see the way in which the aesthetic entails a certain ethical dimension. One can trace a great deal of what has happened in art, architecture and aesthetics in the twentieth century back to developments at the end of the eighteenth century, to Kant's critical philosophy and in particular to his *Third Critique*, where he develops the notion of art as self-referential or non-referential. That understanding of art was appropriated by a thinker like Schiller, for instance, in his famous text of 1794 'Letters and The Aesthetic Education of Man.' Kant's notion of self-referentiality is the philosophical articulation of what becomes the doctrine of art as being about art, rather than being about something else. Schiller accepts Kant's notion of art as non-referential or self-referential, but says that art is not about that which one hangs on the wall or sits on a pedestal, but must be embodied in the world. The world must be transformed into a work of art. This ideal once was realized in Ancient Greece, but was lost in the industrial age when the harmony of this original condition gave way to fragmentation and alienation. For Schiller and the Romantics, the task of the artist was to transform the world into a work of art by achieving this condition of harmony, unity and synthesis. This is a three part story: an original condition, a fall into opposition and separation, and a movement toward some kind of utopia. The one who is going to lead us from this fallen condition into that utopia is the artist. Hence the notion of aesthetic education.

The other thing that is obviously going on during this period is that art is coming to displace religion; the artist is now playing the role that the religious prophet played previously. Schiller's formulation of the task of the artist is where you really begin to get the articulation of what becomes the avant-garde in this century. From the Russian constructivists and the Bauhaus to Mies' importation of the Bauhaus and technology, the challenge is to transform the world into a work of art. This point of view runs very deeply throughout the Modernist tradition. In so far as art has that kind of social and political program, it has an undeniable ethical dimension. Thus, the aesthetic and the ethical are interrelated in Modernism.

Now what does that mean for what you as architects and architecture students do today? Part of what it means is that you have to think critically and reflectively about what kind of ethical engagement your aesthetic principles entail. In creating different spaces you not only are creating an aesthetic space but are also creating different conditions for being and being-in-the-world. Instead of seeing ethics and aesthetics as somehow oppositional or inversely related, we have come to see the way in which the aesthetic is inseparably bound up with the ethical; in formulating aesthetic principals or creating aesthetic objects, one is unavoidably engaged in an ethical kind of gesture or act.

We are at a moment of extraordinarily important social, political, and economic transition. It is described in many ways: there is a shift from Modernism to Post-Modernism, from industrial capitalism to informational capitalism. Part of what is going on is that the distinctions and oppositions that we have used to interpret the world and to structure experience for a long time, oppositions that go back as far as Plato, are beginning to unravel. This is a function of what is known as the information revolution. But in order to appreciate the stakes of this change, you must realize that information is not merely something that is bound to the computer, rather information processes characterize multiple dimensions of experience – from the social and the political to the economic and even the biological. In important ways it is obvious that economic processes are information processes. This is significant because it calls into question the traditional interpretative opposition of superstructure and infrastructure. If one were working within the Marxist analysis of economic processes, it would be necessary to make a distinction between the ideological superstructure processes on the one hand, and the material infrastructure processes on the other. However, those infrastructure processes are in fact informational processes. As is now increasingly obvious, the very distinction between superstructure – symbols and logic – and infrastructure unravels. You no longer have the same kind of foundational structure, which allows the superstructure to be reduced to infrastructure. When both are information, you have the reversibility of the code, and can't privilege one over the other. Either can be read through the other.

One can also extend that same kind of distinction or analysis to biological or natural processes. What once appeared to be material biological processes are now understood as informational processes. Consequently, the whole relationship between mind and matter, or the material and the immaterial, is confounded. If biological processes are informational processes, the relationship between nature and culture cannot be as oppositional as it has been taken to be. It is basically the distinction between form and matter. Matter is not as material as we once thought it was, and now increasingly appears to be immaterial. Here we have a reversibility of the code in terms of natural processes. To put it differently, interpretative processes cannot be reductive if the code is reversible: you can't reduce nature to culture any-more than you can reduce culture to nature. One of the criticisms of information and virtual technologies that is repeatedly made is that they involve a forgetting of, a repression of the body and material conditions. I think it is a mistake to understand the virtual in opposition to the so-called material. Nietzsche somewhere says that when reality goes, we are not left with appearance because appearance and reality are a package deal, each is defined in constituting in and through the other. There-fore when one goes, the other is transformed. The virtual involves a complication of oppositions. This is clear in many of the projects. These works extend the inter-face beyond the screen in a way that enables us to inhabit an interface culture. The so-called realities with which we deal are virtual so that virtuality becomes a kind of reality. But reality now is not what it was in the pre-virtual condition.

Part of what Hani is trying to do is to place us in this virtual condition. His Stock Exchange Project, for instance, attempts to reproduce what the stock exchange floor looks like in a virtual environment. A more interesting question is how can one inhabit information differently by the construction or articulation of virtual spaces? In relation to Hani's Guggenheim project, one of the questions to be pressed is how can the virtual Guggenheim enrich the experience of art differently than a visit to the non-virtual or 'real' Guggenheim? I think it is fascinating that his two major projects so far are the Stock Exchange on the one hand, and the Guggenheim on the other. This is interesting because in a certain sense one of the ways to understand what has been happening over the past thirty years is that economics is becoming more and more a matter of image, and image is becoming more and more a matter of econom-ics. Art and economics in other words are on a sliding continuum.

The work that Greg is doing with his students is intriguing in many ways. It represents both continuity and discontinuity with past architecture. The discontinuity is obvious: in recent years software has transformed the work of many younger architects. Someone like Frank Gehry could not build what he imagined until he had the software to do it. As I understand his work, he still works from models, which he then transfers into designs done on computers. Increasingly though, the architecture being produced is a function of the software that is being used. If you look at the Embryological Houses that Greg does, they are in many ways radically different from anything you have seen. But there is still a commonality between the kind of grid-like structure of Levittown and his module and its variations. I know Greg wants to make a distinction between module and modular and modularization. One of the differences between the modular house you would have in Levittown and the kind that Greg is working on, is that in the grid-like structure and plain box of the Modernist house you can change parts without modifying the whole. In the modularity of Greg's houses, when you change one part, the whole changes; this is a different kind of structure.

The other thing that is fascinating is the way in which Greg consciously and deliberately invokes biological and sexual metaphors and images. We are clearly shifting from machine to organism. If you watch the rhetoric he uses, his favorite adjective is voluptuous. The difference between the machine aesthetic and the voluptuous reflects a more erotic environment. One question is why the logic of these structures should be worked out in terms of the single dwelling and the domestic space. That doesn't necessarily mean that Greg is not interested in extending his analysis to broader issues. Certainly part of what is going on in contemporary culture is a process of globalization through which an infinite web of relations becomes entangled. One does not get as much of a sense of this global context in the isolation of the individual house. I think that what one does have in the Embryological House is a conscious and interesting interplay between interiority and exteriority in so far as there is an effort to modulate the houses in relation to the setting and the environment. But still, the questions remain: why is the concentration on domestic space so important, and what does this have to do with the whole set of terms and issues that focus on a sexuality and domesticity? I think these issues need to be raised.

The other thing that is interesting in terms of continuity and discontinuity with previous architecture is that the work of both Hani and Greg represents a certain break with their 'fathers.' Younger architects are in touch with a different set of sensibilities than the architects who have been dominating the scene for the past decade. And yet there is also an extraordinary continuity in terms of their pedagogical relationships in the studio. Their students are very bright and very interesting: they have a broad range of sensitivities and sensibilities. The way in which the educational process continues to work is basically through apprenticeship. If I were to translate what goes on in the studio to my own work, it would be as if I were to outline the book and then ask my students to write different chapters. I understand of course that one of the ways in which we learn is to apprentice ourselves to a teacher as well as many others. There are thinkers you must think about and those you must think with; those who really teach you are those you think with. Now the parameters for the projects that the students are doing are firmly set by the instructor. On the one hand, the work that is being done represents a significant break from, or an extension of the work that has been done by previous generations. On the other hand, it perpetuates precisely the structure that I know these architects in their late 30s, early 40s find so oppressive about their own experience, because they are still struggling mightily against those to whom they may remain so indebted.

I found very interesting the students' interest in color. Part of the change that is taking place in architecture today is the shift from straight lines and right angles and absence of color to twists, curves and colors. That is a significant change. In terms of the history of Modernism, color, curve, and ornament are associated with the primitive, feminine, infantile, and mad, whereas straight lines, right angles, and the absence of color are associated with the modern, rational, masculine, and mature. These aesthetic principals are coded in ways that carry significant ethical and political weight.

One of the student projects I found very suggestive is the one in which the students are trying to develop a floor system. They have developed a floor system by basically taking a running shoe and inverting it. That was an instance where the students were thinking outside the box that Greg had created for them.

The Embryological House is most interesting in so far as it represents a logic different from mechanical structures. For this logic to be as compelling as it could be, Greg has to expand the problem beyond the single dwelling in terms of the broader social, political, and economic context. For instance, what would it be like to extend the principles of this kind of project to Levittown? How would a community or a neighborhood or a section of a city that would be designed for the principles of the house differ from the way in which cities and neighborhoods work now? I think that complex, non-linear dynamics, or to put it in different terms, the kind of principles of what some theorists call 'complex adaptive systems' are at work in the Embryological House. But those principles are characteristic not simply or most interestingly of the single dwelling but of the overall context. One can argue that there is some kind of fractal structure characteristic of the single dwelling, which is also characteristic of a larger context.

From my point of view many of these different strands are interrelated. It is not just the economic, the political, and the social but the philosophical, the religious, and the aesthetic that interrelate to create the context in which we live and think. I think that students are not adequately exposed to these intersections. When they begin to get some sense of the subtle ways in which religion, philosophy, and science inform contemporary cultural practices, they reach a deeper understanding not only of the history and the context in which they do the things that they do but also the implications of what they are doing. They come to understand and appreciate that what they are doing is not simply a variation of architectural practice but involves a whole set of values and philosophical ideals, which lead to ethical commitments that are made implicitly or explicitly in the design decisions. If they are to understand what they are doing, they must think critically and reflectively about the stakes of those decisions and why they make the choices they make.

Biographies

Max Hollein is the artistic and administrative Director of the Schirn Kunsthalle in Frankfurt. He worked at the Guggenheim Museum in New York from 1995 to 2000 where he held the position of Chief of Staff and Manager of European Relations. He was the US Commissioner and Curator for the VII Architecture Biennale in Venice in 2000. Besides his book *Zeitgenössische Kunst und der Kunstmarktboom* he has been editor of and contributor to several periodical publications, books and exhibition catalogues. Max Hollein holds masters' degrees in art history and business administration.

Greg Lynn FORM was established in 1994 in Hoboken, NJ and relocated to Venice, California in 1998 to take advantage of the design and manufacturing techniques germane to the aeronautic, automobile and film industries of Southern California. The office is working on projects of radically disparate scales; from the PGLIFE Showroom (Stockholm) and Uniserve Corporate Headquarters (Los Angeles) to the Korean Presbyterian Church (NYC) and a massive 500 unit housing project (Bijlmermeer, Amsterdam). They were just commissioned to design the Ark of the World Museum in the mountainous rainforests of Costa Rica. Because of his early combination of degrees in philosophy and architecture, Greg Lynn has been involved in combining the realities of design and construction with the speculative, theoretical and experimental potentials of writing and teaching. For three years he was a Professor at the ETH in Zurich and throughout the 1990's he taught at Columbia University. He just accepted a Professorship at the 'Angewandte' in Vienna and for the last four years he has been a Studio Professor at UCLA in Los Angeles and the Davenport Professor at Yale University. He is the author of *Folds, Bodies and Blobs: Collected Essays, Folding in Architecture and Animate Form*. He graduated from Miami University of Ohio with degrees in both architecture and philosophy and later from Princeton University where he received a graduate degree in architecture.

Hani Rashid is an Adjunct Associate Professor of Architecture at Columbia University in New York, and has taught architecture and lectured throughout Europe and the United States. In 1989, he, along with partner Lise Anne Couture, formed Asymptote, a design, architecture and research practice based in New York City. Asymptote has produced a number of key works in recent years that involve the use of digital tools and technologies in their conception and outcome. Among the most important are the 3DTF, a virtual reality trading floor designed for the New York Stock Exchange, and the Guggenheim Virtual Museum, a project commissioned by the Solomon R. Guggenheim Museum to incorporate and house their digital and Internet related art collections. Most recently Asymptote has completed the construction of HydraPier, a permanent building housing technology and art in Holland near Schiphol airport, an installation entitled Flux 3.0 MotionScapes at Documenta XI, a new line of office furniture for Knoll International, and *Flux*, a survey of their recent work published by Phaidon Press Limited.

Mark C. Taylor is the Cluett Professor of Humanities at Williams College. He received a Doktorgrad (Philosophy) from the University of Copenhagen in 1981, a Ph.D. from Harvard in 1973, and a B.A. from Wesleyan University in 1968. Professor Taylor has written numerous books and articles on a variety of topics, from tattoos to architecture, to theology and creating global classrooms. He has collaborated on works in a variety of media, including CD ROM and film. Some of his works include: *Erring: A Postmodern A/Theology* (University of Chicago, 1984); *Disfiguring: Art, Architecture, Religion* (University of Chicago, 1992); *Imagologies: Media Philosophy* (Routledge, 1994); *The Picture in Question: Mark Tansey and the Ends of Representation* (University of Chicago, 1999); *The Moment of Complexity: Emerging Network Culture* (University of Chicago Press, 2001); *Grave Matters* (Reaktion, 2002). His exhibition, *Grave Matters*, opens at the Massachusetts Museum of Contemporary art in the fall of 2002. In 1997 Taylor co-founded the Global Education Network (GEN), which is a web-based company that develops the highest quality college-level courses in the humanities, liberal arts, social sciences, and sciences, and distributes them online for an affordable price. Taylor has received many awards including the Distinguished Alumnus Award from Wesleyan University, the Carnegie Foundation for the Advancement of Teaching National College Professor of the Year award, the Rector's Medal from the University of Helsinki, and the American Academy of Religion Award for Excellence for his books *Nots* and *Altarity*.

COMA is an interdisciplinary studio for art, design and media, based in Amsterdam and New York, founded by Cornelia Blatter and Marcel Hermans. COMA has designed books, magazines, corporate IDs and posters for various publishers and museums in the USA and Europe. Recent books include *Rietveld in Utrecht* for the Centraal Museum in Utrecht; the *Hugo Boss Prize 2002* for the Guggenheim Museum in New York; and *Relocated: Twenty Sculptures by Isamu Noguchi from Japan* for the Noguchi Garden Museum in New York. COMA also produces its own multiples and editions, independent art projects. The studio was an ID Magazine Design Review winner in 2000 and was nominated for the Rotterdam Design Prize in 2001.

Véronique Patteeuw has degrees in architecture and cultural studies. She collaborated at the architectural program of Brussels2000, European Cultural Capital, and was secretary of the network Studio Open City. Currently she is working as an editor for NAi Publishers in Rotterdam, where she develops books on architecture and urban planning. Most recently, she co-founded A16, a platform focussing on young architects in Belgium.

Credits

The student research projects presented in this book, were developed during the exhibition 'Lynn/Rashid: Architectural Laboratories' with Columbia University, New York and UCLA, Los Angeles. This exhibition has been developed by Max Hollein, US Commissioner, in association with The Solomon R. Guggenheim Foundation.

The program was sponsored by IBM IntelliStation, Chrysler Italia, 3M, Delta Air Lines, Zero Systemic Furniture, and BTicino. Generous support was provided by Precix Advanced Cutting Technologies, Panasonic Italia, RAS, Walter Lantz Foundation, and William Kinne Fellows Trust. Additional support was provided by Kaindl Flooring, Zumtobel Staff, Bisazza, Dietl International Services, Alias|Wavefront, Gladys Krieble Delmas Foundation, Bruno and Christina Bischofberger, Trivioquadrivio, an anonymous donor, and Intrapresae Collezione Guggenheim.

Architectural Laboratories
Greg Lynn with UCLA, Los Angeles
Plastic Flowers
Michelle Cintron, Jennifer Williams, Anne Rosenberg, Sara Weinstein
Tadpoles
Paul Andersen, Jeff McKibban, Dan Riley
X-Ray Wall System
Elena Manferdini, Patrick McEneany, Cynthia Bush, Brooke Williams
Tongue
Mark Rea Baker, Rahul Gore, Daksh Shani

Soft Ball Project
Ryan Brooke Thomas, Maria-Jose Riera, Jeremy Schacht, Amanda Salud-Gallivan
Responsive Floor System
Mario Cipresso, Alison Buddlemeyer, Paul Tran

GL Form Projects
Eyebeam Museum of Art and Technology
GL Form with SOM and reasonsense, Elena Manferdini, Jackilin Hah
Extension of St. Gallen Kunstmuseum
GL Form, Elena Manferdini, Maria Florencia Pita, Patrick McEneany, Nathalie Rhinne, Stefan Hoerner, Jackilin Hah, Nuri Miller
Rendel + Spitz Bleb Prototype 1
GL Form, Oliver Bertram, Marcelyn Gow, Stefan Hoerner, Sven Neumann, Nathalie Rhinne, Martina von Tippel Skirch
Numinous Ceilings
GL Form, Elena Manferdini, Patrick McEneany, Stefan Hoerner, Nathalie Rhinne
Visionaire #34 Case Design
GL Form, Jackilin Hah
Lords Clothing Store On Sunset
GL Form, Jackilin Hah, Elena Manferdini, Nathalie Rinne, Stefan Hoerner
Transformation of the Kleiburg Housing Block
GL Form, Patrick McEneany, Jackilin Hah, Elena Manferdini, Maria Florencia Pita, Nuri Miller, Chris Kabatsi
Ark of The World
GL Form, Maria Florencia Pita, Elena Manferdini, Chris Kabatsi, Jackilin Hah, Patrick McEneany, Nuri Miller, ArcA San Jose, Costa Rica, Walter Hidalgo Xirinachs

Alessi Tea And Coffee Piazza
GL Form, Elena Manferdini, Patrick McEneany, Claus Dold, Nuri Miller
Predator
GL Form in collaboration with painter Fabian Marcaccio, Elena Manferdini, Amanda Salud-Gallivan, Jackilin, Hah, David Erdman, Jeff Mc Kibban, Dan Riley, Jeremey Schacht, Patrick McEneany
Central Building: BMW Factory Leipzig
GL Form, Jackilin Hah, Patrick McEneany, Elena Manferdini, Maria Florencia Pita, Claus Dold, Nuri Miller
Uniserve Corporate Headquarters
GL Form, Jackilin Hah, Patrick McEneany, Nathalie Rhinne, Elena Manfredini, Stefan Hoerner
Pretty Good Life Showroom
GL Form with Dynamo Sthlm, Stockholm, Jackilin Hah, David Chow
Deitch Projects Chess Set
GL Form with Greg Foley and Donald Hearn, Elena Manferdini, Nuri Miller, Stefan Hoerner

Architectural Laboratories
Hani Rashid with Columbia University, New York
Broadcast Architecture
Nina Bischofberger, Brandon Hicks, Kyungsan Kim, Sangjun Oh, Chutayaves Sinthuphan. Special thanks to: Carlo Zago & Co.
Performance Architecture
David Burns, Paul Preissner, Megumi Tamanaha, Jason Tax, Dragana Zoric. Special thanks to: Elam USA, Inc.
Airport Urbanism
Hui Min Chan, Laura Elvia Hernandez, Lloyd Willem Huber, Maria Papadatou, Arthur Schellenberg

Asymptote Projects
Eyebeam Museum of Art and Technology
Hani Rashid and Lise Anne Couture, Ruth Berktold, John Cleater, Jose Salinas, Noboru Ota, Birgit Schoenbrodt, Renate Weissenboeck, Hannah Yampolsky, Alain Merkli, Moritz Schoendorf
Guggenheim Virtual Museum
Hani Rashid and Lise Anne Couture, John Cleater, Noboru Ota, David Serero, Florian Pfeifer, Ruth Ron, Birgit Schoenbrodt
BMW Event and Delivery Center
Hani Rashid and Lise Anne Couture, Florencia Maria Pita, Ruth Berktold, Birgit Schoenbrodt, Noboru Ota, Ruth Ron, Renate Weissenboeck, Hannah Yampolsky, Alain Merkli, Moritz Schoendorf
New York Stock Exchange Ramp
Hani Rashid and Lise Anne Couture, John Cleater, Elaine Didyk, Samuel Hassler, Sabine Muller, Folker Kleinekort, Marcos Velasques, Kevin Estrada, Henning Meyer, Carlos Ballestri
Stream House
Hani Rashid and Lise Anne Couture
NYSE 3DTF Virtual Reality Environment
Hani Rashid and Lise Anne Couture, John Cleater, Elaine Didyk, Samuel Hassler, Sabine Muller, Folker Kleinekort, Marcos Velasques, Kevin Estrada, Henning Meyer, Carlos Ballestri
Fluxspace 1.0 Installation
Hani Rashid and Lise Anne Couture, Ruth Berkhold, John Cleater, Noboru Ota, Florian Pfeifer

Fluxspace 2.0 Pavilion
Hani Rashid and Lise Anne
Couture, John Cleater, Noboru
Ota, Florian Pfeifer
I. Scapes Installation
Hani Rashid and Lise Anne
Couture, John Cleater, David
Serero, Kevin Estrada, Katrin
Kalden, Remo Burkhard
Airport Urbanism
Hani Rashid and Lise Anne
Couture, Herman Zschiegner,
Birgit Schoenbrodt
Flux 3.0/ Mscapes
Hani Rashid and Lise Anne
Couture, John Cleater,
Noboru Ota
Hydra-Pier
Hani Rashid and Lise Anne
Couture, Elaine Didyk, Birgit
Schoenbrodt, Jose Salinas, John
Cleater, Gemma Koppen, Martin
Thue Jacobsen, Alain Merkli,
Moritz Schoendorf, Rafal Bajuk

Credits Illustrations
Page 10 - 81
All images are copyright Greg
Lynn FORM with the exception of
Page 20, 21, 41, photo: Marvin
Rand
Page 23, photo: Martin Rendel
Page 40, photo: Brandon Welling
Page 76, photo: Dan Forbes
Page 92 - 167
All images are copyright
Asymptote with the exception of:
Page 120 - 121, photo: Asymp-
tote/ SIAC/ NYSE
Page 160 - 165, photo: Christian
Richters
Page 1-7, 10-11, 16-17, 24-25,
32-33, 42-43, 52-53, 62-63, 70-
71, 82-93, 100-101, 124-125,
144-145, 166-167, 174-176
All images are copyright
The Solomon R. Guggenheim
Foundation

Acknowledgements

Text and Images
Greg Lynn and Hani Rashid
Compiled and Edited by
Véronique Patteeuw
Copy Editing
D'Laine Camp, Rotterdam
Concept and Design
COMA, Amsterdam/New York
coma@aya.yale.edu
Special thanks to
Marion Pot, Elena Manferdini,
Patrick McEneany and
Christin Minotte
Lithography and Printing
Die Keure, Bruges
Publisher
Simon Franke

NAi Publishers is an inter-
nationally orientated publisher
specialized in developing,
producing and distributing
books on architecture, visual
arts and related disciplines.
www.naipublishers.nl
info@naipublishers.nl

© NAi Publishers, Rotterdam,
2002

Available in North, South and
Central America through D.A.P./
Distributed Art Publishers Inc,
155 Sixth Avenue 2nd Floor,
New York, NY 10013-1507, Tel
212 6271999, Fax 212 6279484.

Available in the United Kingdom
and Ireland through Art Data,
12 Bell Industrial Estate, 50
Cunnington Street, London W4
5HB, Tel 208 7471061, Fax 208
7422319.

Printed and Bound in Belgium
ISBN 90-5662-241-2